K9

The *Pocket*
TREE
EXPER
Dr. D. G. Hessayon

D0511713

First edition: 150,000 copies
Published 2001
by Expert Books
a division of Transworld Publishers

Copyright © Dr.D.G.Hessayon 2001

The right of Dr.D.G.Hessayon to be identified
as author of this work has been asserted in accordance
with sections 77 and 78 of the Copyright Designs and
Patents Act 1988.

A catalogue record for this book is available from the British Library

TRANSWORLD PUBLISHERS
61-63 Uxbridge Road, London W5 5SA
a division of the Random House Group Ltd

 Distributed in the United States
by Sterling Publishing Co. Inc.,
387 Park Avenue South,
New York,
NY 10016-8810

EXPERT BOOKS

CONTENTS

Reproduction by Spot On Digital Imaging Ltd, Perivale, Middx. UB6 7JB
Printed and bound by GGP Media GmbH

ISBN 0 903505 56 8   © D.G. HESSAYON 2001

CHAPTER 1

INTRODUCTION

The first Tree & Shrub Expert appeared nearly 20 years ago, but there is no need to change the opening paragraph in this Pocket edition — "Gardening styles may come and gardening styles may go, but ornamental trees and shrubs go on for ever". In the 1980s there was the container boom with potted shrubs and small trees providing focal points around the garden. Towards the end of the 1990s came the hard landscaping craze, with our magazines and TV screens filled with garden makeovers of glass, gravel, water, stone and brightly-painted wood.

Despite the new fashions nearly all our gardens remain essentially unaltered — areas of grass with beds and borders filled with plants. Among these plants the woody ones — the shrubs, trees, climbers and conifers — have a vital part to play. They create the upright living framework of the garden. In summer they provide height, colour and fragrance — they give the garden its shape. In winter their role is just as important. When the plants in the flower garden have died down, the bare branches of the deciduous (leaf-losing) shrubs and trees and the leaf-covered stems of the evergreens ensure that we are looking at a garden bed or border and not a bare patch of ground.

The bewildering array of plants at the garden centre have a wide range of needs, heights, flowering times, pruning requirements etc. Over the years millions of gardeners have turned to The Tree & Shrub Expert for advice. Now there is a Pocket edition, designed to be taken into the garden, shop or garden centre to provide on-the-spot information.

The basic style has been retained but the text has been boiled down to the essential bare facts. All the popular genera have been retained together with many unusual ones, but rarities listed in only a few catalogues have been omitted.

Boiled down to basics, but not over-simplified. The soil and light needs of each plant together with its pruning requirements are dealt with in some detail rather than being left to a few symbols. Take this Pocket Expert with you to the garden centre or nursery and check the basic facts before you buy — a well-grown and well-chosen tree or shrub will repay many times over the money and care you have bestowed on it.

PLANT TYPES

There are four basic groups of woody plants — shrubs, trees, climbers and conifers. Shrubs with their vast range of colours and sizes are the most popular, and even a modest collection can give you flowers all year round. Conifers are also popular and are chosen for their shape rather than their colour. Trees are bought in fewer numbers as the average-sized garden can house very few, but their architectural value should not be overlooked. On the other hand the importance of climbers for clothing walls, fences and arches is known to everyone.

CLIMBER

A climber is a perennial plant which has the ability to attach itself to or twine around an upright structure. This climbing habit may not develop until the plant is established.

Several shrubs, such as Firethorn, Winter Jasmine and Flowering Quince are not true climbers but they are commonly grown against walls and trellis-work.

SHRUB

A shrub is a perennial plant which bears several woody stems at or close to ground level. A mature shrub may be only 5 cm high or as tall as 7 m. Usually chosen for its foliage and/or flowers rather than its shape.

The dividing line between trees and shrubs is not really clear-cut. Several shrubs, such as Holly, Flowering Dogwood and Hazel may grow as small trees.

TREE

A tree is a perennial plant which bears only one woody stem at ground level. A mature tree may be only 60 cm high or as tall as 30 m or more, depending on the variety.

CONIFER

A conifer is a perennial plant which bears cones. These cones are nearly always made up of woody scales, but there are exceptions (e.g Yew). The leaves are usually evergreen but there are exceptions (e.g Larch).

Shape is an extremely important consideration when choosing trees and conifers. A columnar tree is a good choice where space is limited or where a specimen plant is required for a small lawn. Where space permits both round-headed and open trees are picturesque and in all gardens conical, pyramidal and weeping trees make excellent focal points.

Size is even more important than shape. A common mistake is to buy a plant which is far too vigorous for the space available — chopping back every year means that both natural beauty and floral display can be lost. In the A-Z guide you will find the height you can expect after 10 years.

COLUMNAR (FASTIGIATE)

CONICAL

PYRAMIDAL

ROUND-HEADED

OPEN

WEEPING (PENDULOUS)

PROSTRATE

GLOBULAR (ROUND)

HORIZONTALLY-BRANCHED

PLANT TYPE
See pages 4-5 for definitions.
More than one type may be
listed — the form you are
most likely to see in the
garden appears first

SPECIES or VARIETY
Where the genus is complex a
single example of each
popular group may be listed.
Ⓓ, (SE) or Ⓔ indicate that there
are deciduous, semi-evergreen
or evergreen varieties

BACKGROUND
Brief notes on the genus —
popularity, plant description,
ease of cultivation etc

FLOWER TIME
Flowering period in
an average season

PRUNING
Look up number 2 on
the inside back cover

GENUS

**COMMON
NAME**

ARBUTUS

Shrub
•
Tree

*A. unedo
'Rubra'*

A. unedo
Strawberry Tree

Grow the most popular
species A. unedo for autumn
and winter interest. Clusters of
pendent flowers appear when
the ripening fruits of last year's
flowers are present.

VARIETIES
Ⓔ

A. unedo – 2 m. White. Slow-
growing — eventually reaches 4 m.
Plant both male and female
specimens for fruit production.

A. u. 'Rubra' – 1.5 m. Pink/white.
Less hardy than the species.

A. andrachnoides – 2 m. White.
Grown for its attractive red bark
rather than its flowers.

FLOWER TIME
October — December

PRUNING
2   Early spring

SITE & SOIL
10

PROPAGATION
5

PROPAGATION
Look up number 5 on the
inside back cover for
details. 1/10 would mean
use either method 1 or
10

FLOWER COLOUR
'Pink/white' means that each
bloom has pink and white
colouring. 'Pink or white' would
mean there are both pink and
white varieties

SITE & SOIL
Look up number 10 on
the inside front cover for
details of the sun, soil
and drainage needs of
the plant

HEIGHT
Anticipated height after
10 years. For climbers
and trailers denotes length
of stem

ABELIA

Shrub

A. grandiflora

SITE & SOIL
2

PROPAGATION
1

A. grandiflora
Abelia

The prolonged flowering period makes this shrub worth growing — some but not all are hardy enough for the average garden. Tubular flowers are borne in clusters.

VARIETIES   Ⓓ or ⓈⒺ

A. grandiflora – 2 m. Pink-tinted white. Arching branches.
A. g. 'Francis Mason' – 1.5 m. Popular yellow-leaved variety.
A. floribunda – 1.5 m. Red. June.
A. 'Edward Goucher' – 1.2 m. Lilac-pink. Semi-evergreen as above.
A. schumannii – 1.2 m. Rose-lilac. The deciduous one. Rather tender.

FLOWER TIME
June — October

PRUNING
2   May

ABELIOPHYLLUM

Shrub

A. distichum

SITE & SOIL
2

PROPAGATION
1/3

A. distichum
White Forsythia

An open bush which has an untidy growth habit and is less leafy than its popular yellow-flowered relative, but it does flower earlier. Best trained against a sunny wall or fence.

VARIETIES   Ⓓ

A. distichum – 1.5 m. Mauve fading to pink and then white. Star-shaped 1 cm flowers appear on bare purple-tinged stems — strong almond-like fragrance. Slender 5 cm long pale green leaves appear when flowering is over.
A. d. 'Roseum' – 1.5 m. Pink flowers. Not easy to find.

FLOWER TIME
February — March

PRUNING
3   After flowering

ABIES

Conifer

A. alba

SITE & SOIL
2

PROPAGATION
5

A. balsamea 'Hudsonia'
Silver Fir

Most are Xmas tree-like and grow too tall for the ordinary garden. The strap-shaped leaves have a sucker-like base and are usually white or grey underneath.

VARIETIES   Ⓔ

A. alba – 3 m; 30 m when mature. Common Silver Fir.
A. koreana – 2 m. Dark green leaves. Purple cones. Popular.
A. balsamea 'Hudsonia' – 30 cm. Rounded dwarf. Popular rock garden variety. Cone-free.
A. arizonica 'Compacta' – 60 cm; 2 m when mature. Blue-grey leaves.

FLOWER TIME
—

PRUNING
1

ABUTILON

Abutilon

Shrub

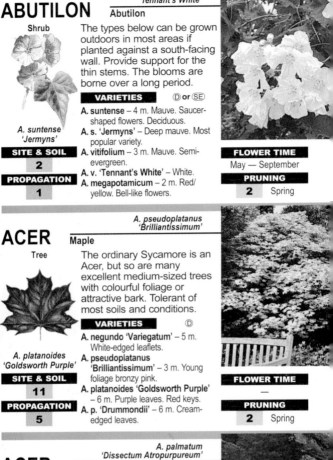

A. vitifolium
'Tennant's White'

The types below can be grown outdoors in most areas if planted against a south-facing wall. Provide support for the thin stems. The blooms are borne over a long period.

A. suntense
'Jermyns'

VARIETIES   Ⓓ or Ⓢⓔ

A. suntense – 4 m. Mauve. Saucer-shaped flowers. Deciduous.
A. s. 'Jermyns' – Deep mauve. Most popular variety.
A. vitifolium – 3 m. Mauve. Semi-evergreen.
A. v. 'Tennant's White' – White.
A. megapotamicum – 2 m. Red/yellow. Bell-like flowers.

SITE & SOIL
2

PROPAGATION
1

FLOWER TIME
May — September

PRUNING
2   Spring

ACER

Maple

Tree

A. pseudoplatanus
'Brilliantissimum'

The ordinary Sycamore is an Acer, but so are many excellent medium-sized trees with colourful foliage or attractive bark. Tolerant of most soils and conditions.

A. platanoides
'Goldsworth Purple'

VARIETIES   Ⓓ

A. negundo 'Variegatum' – 5 m. White-edged leaflets.
A. pseudoplatanus 'Brilliantissimum' – 3 m. Young foliage bronzy pink.
A. platanoides 'Goldsworth Purple' – 6 m. Purple leaves. Red keys.
A. p. 'Drummondii' – 6 m. Cream-edged leaves.

SITE & SOIL
11

PROPAGATION
5

FLOWER TIME
—

PRUNING
2   Spring

ACER

Japanese Maple

Shrub

A. palmatum
'Dissectum Atropurpureum'

Most Acers are trees — see above. The Japanese Maples, however, are slow-growing shrubs with attractive leaves. Provide shelter and protect from morning sun.

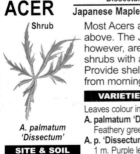

A. palmatum
'Dissectum'

VARIETIES   Ⓓ

Leaves colour in autumn:
A. palmatum 'Dissectum' – 1 m. Feathery green leaves turn orange.
A. p. 'Dissectum Atropurpureum' – 1 m. Purple leaves turn red-purple.
A. p. 'Osakazuki' – 2 m. Green leaves turn bright red.
A. japonicum 'Aureum' – 1 m. Yellow leaves turn orange.

SITE & SOIL
6

PROPAGATION
5

FLOWER TIME
—

PRUNING
2   Spring

8

ACTINIDIA

A. chinensis

Actinidia

Climber

A. kolomikta

The most popular species is grown for its colourful leaves. Others are planted for their floral display or edible fruit. With fruiting types plant both a male and female specimen.

VARIETIES   (D)

A. kolomikta – 5 m. White. June. Red- and cream-tipped leaves. Small flowers are followed by egg-shaped fruits.

A. chinensis – 8 m. Cream. July-August. Kiwi Fruit. Large heart-shaped leaves. Grown for its brown, furry fruits — needs a good summer to mature.

SITE & SOIL
12

PROPAGATION
2

FLOWER TIME
Depends on species

PRUNING
2   Winter

AESCULUS

A. pavia

Horse Chestnut

Tree
•
Shrub

A. hippocastanum

The Common Horse Chestnut is a fine sight when in full flower in May, but it is far too large for most gardens. Choose instead one of the Shrubby Horse Chestnuts.

VARIETIES   (D)

A. hippocastanum – 25 m when mature. White candles. May. Common Horse Chestnut.

A. carnea 'Briotii' – 6 m when mature. Red candles. May.

A. parviflora – 3 m. White bottle brushes. July-August.

A. pavia – 3 m. Red candles. July. Red Buckeye.

SITE & SOIL
11

PROPAGATION
6/7

FLOWER TIME
Depends on species

PRUNING
2   Early spring

AILANTHUS

A. altissima

Tree of Heaven

Tree

A. altissima

A fanciful name for a handsome, large-leaved tree. It is quick-growing, reaching 20 m at maturity. Suckers freely, which can be a nuisance in a small garden. Tolerates polluted air.

VARIETIES   (D)

A. altissima – 14 m. Greenish-yellow inconspicuous male and female flowers are borne on separate trees. Female trees bear bunches of orange key-like fruits. Ash-like leaves grow up to 1 m long — they turn yellow in autumn. Some annual die-back is normal. The only species you are likely to find.

SITE & SOIL
10

PROPAGATION
8

FRUITING TIME
September

PRUNING
4   Spring

AKEBIA

Climber

A. quinata

A. quinata

Akebia

A vigorous twiner which will quite quickly cover a dead tree or south-facing wall. Masses of small blooms appear in spring — sausage-shaped fruits occasionally develop.

VARIETIES (SE)

A. quinata – 7 m. Red-purple. Drooping flower-heads are followed by brown-purple fruits if summer has been hot and dry. Leaves are made up of 5 oval leaflets. The only species you are likely to find.

A. trifoliata – 10 m. Dark purple. Violet fruits. Leaves are made up of 3 leaflets.

SITE & SOIL
3

PROPAGATION
6

FLOWER TIME
April — May

PRUNING
2   After flowering

ALNUS

Tree

A. incana

A. cordata

Alder

A good choice if you need a fast-growing hedge in a boggy part of the garden — not generally suitable for chalky soil. Conical shape with attractive catkins in spring.

VARIETIES (D)

A. glutinosa – 10 m. Catkins 10 cm long. Common Alder. Dark green glossy leaves.

A. g. 'Aurea' – 6 m. Yellow leaves.

A. incana – 12 m. Catkins 7 cm long. Grey Alder. Leaves grey below.

A. cordata – 12 m. Catkins 5 cm long. Italian Alder. Glossy leaves. Tolerates chalky soil.

SITE & SOIL
13

PROPAGATION
3

FLOWER TIME
March — April

PRUNING
2   Spring

AMELANCHIER

Tree
•
Shrub

A. canadensis

A. canadensis

Snowy Mespilus

A tree or large shrub grown for its changing display. Coppery foliage and white flowers in spring, red berries in summer and orange-red leaves in autumn.

VARIETIES (D)

A. canadensis – 6 m. White. Small, starry flowers in erect clusters. Red berries ripen to black. The most popular species.

A. lamarckii – Pink leaves in spring.

A. grandiflora 'Ballerina' – 4 m. White. Larger flowers than A. canadensis. Compact growth habit.

A. g. 'Rubescens' – 6 m. Pink.

SITE & SOIL
10

PROPAGATION
8

FLOWER TIME
April — May

PRUNING
2   Late winter

ANDROMEDA

A. polifolia
Andromeda

Shrub

A good companion for Rhododendron and other acid lovers. The open bush bears 0.5 cm white or pink bells hanging in clusters from the tips of the branches.

A. polifolia

VARIETIES Ⓓ

A. polifolia – 45 cm. Bog Rosemary. Bluish-green leaves, white below. The only species you will find.
A. p. 'Compacta' – 30 cm. Pink.
A. p. 'Minima' – 25 cm. Pink. Prostrate matted growth.
A. p. 'Alba' – 15 cm. White.
A. p. 'Macrophylla' – 10 cm. White/pink. Useful rockery type.

| SITE & SOIL |
| 14 |

| PROPAGATION |
| 4 |

| FLOWER TIME |
| May — June |

| PRUNING | |
| 2 | Late autumn |

ARALIA

A. elata 'Variegata'
Japanese Angelica

Shrub

A large shrub which suckers freely — give it the space it needs. Each leaf is 1 m long, neatly divided into a complex pattern of leaflets. Choose a sheltered site.

A. elata 'Aureovariegata'

VARIETIES Ⓓ

A. elata – 3 m. White. Large branching heads of tiny flowers. Thorny twisted branches. The only species you are likely to find.
A. e. 'Variegata' – 2.5 m. White. Leaves cream-edged in spring.
A. e. 'Aureovariegata' – 2.5 m. White. Leaves yellow-edged in spring — changing to silvery-white.

| SITE & SOIL |
| 3 |

| PROPAGATION |
| 5 |

| FLOWER TIME |
| August — September |

| PRUNING | |
| 2 | Spring |

ARAUCARIA

A. araucana
Monkey Puzzle Tree

Conifer

Easy to recognise — thick, sharply-pointed leaves are arranged spirally around each branch. Grows very slowly at first, but then grows rapidly to reach 20 m or more.

A. araucana

VARIETIES Ⓔ

A. araucana – 1.2 m. Glossy dark green leaves. Thick curved branches. Globular 15 cm cones are borne on upper branches of female trees. Male trees bear clusters of brown catkins. Growth is conical at first — later round-topped. Buy a container-grown tree and plant in a sheltered site.

| SITE & SOIL |
| 3 |

| PROPAGATION |
| 5 |

| FLOWER TIME |
| — |

| PRUNING |
| 1 |

ARBUTUS

Strawberry Tree

A. unedo

Shrub • Tree

A. unedo 'Rubra'

Grow the most popular species A. unedo for autumn and winter interest. Clusters of pendent flowers appear when the ripening fruits of last year's flowers are present.

VARIETIES Ⓔ

A. unedo – 2 m. White. Slow-growing — eventually reaches 4 m. Plant both male and female specimens for fruit production.

A. u. 'Rubra' – 1.5 m. Pink/white. Less hardy than the species.

A. andrachnoides – 2 m. White. Grown for its attractive red bark rather than its flowers.

SITE & SOIL
10

PROPAGATION
5

FLOWER TIME
October — December

PRUNING
2   Early spring

ARCTOSTAPHYLOS

Bearberry

A. uva-ursi

Shrub

A. uva-ursi

You can try this evergreen ground cover if you like to grow unusual plants, but it will only succeed if the soil is acid and the site is sunny. Useful for a sandy, lime-free bank.

VARIETIES Ⓔ

A. uva-ursi – 30 cm. Pink-tipped white. Red Bearberry. Flowers are followed by red glossy berries in autumn. Mat-like growth of slender branches, eventually reaching 1 m spread. The only species you are likely to find.

A. nevadensis – 30 cm. Pink-tipped white. Less hardy than A. uva-ursi.

SITE & SOIL
9

PROPAGATION
9

FLOWER TIME
April

PRUNING
2   Late winter

ARUNDINARIA

Bamboo

A. viridistriata

Shrub

A. nitida

Bamboos are becoming increasingly popular as focal points and for screening. Many have an exotic look but they are quite easy to grow. Provide some shelter.

VARIETIES Ⓔ

A. murieliae – 3 m. Yellow stems.
A. nitida – 3 m. Purple stems.
A. palmata – 3 m. Long leaves.
A. fastuosa – 6 m. Very tall stems.
A. viridistriata – 1.5 m. Yellow-striped leaves. Purplish-green stems.
A. variegata – 1 m. Cream-striped leaves.

SITE & SOIL
15

PROPAGATION
10

FLOWER TIME
—

PRUNING
5   Spring

12

AUCUBA

Shrub

A. japonica 'Variegata'

A. japonica 'Picturata'

Aucuba

A popular choice when looking for an evergreen with large colourful leaves for a shady spot. A 'grow-anywhere' plant, but new growth may be scorched by icy winds.

VARIETIES Ⓔ

A. japonica – 2 m. All-green. Variety may be male (M) or female (F).
A. j. 'Longifolia' – (F) Narrow leaves.
A. j. 'Variegata' – (F) Yellow-splashed leaves.
A. j. 'Golden King' – (M) Yellow-splashed leaves.
A. j. 'Picturata' – (M) Yellow-centred.
A. j. 'Rozannie' – (M/F) Self-fertile.

SITE & SOIL
16

PROPAGATION
1/3

BERRY TIME
September — January

PRUNING
2   May

AZARA

Shrub

A. dentata

A. microphylla

Azara

Not popular as it needs a sheltered wall and is too tall for many gardens, but an attractive tree-like bush in the right situation. Fluffy flowers are borne in clusters.

VARIETIES Ⓔ

A. microphylla – 4 m. Yellow. March. The fragrant blooms are borne on the underside of the branches — stamens rather than petals provide the display.
A. m. 'Variegata' – Yellow-edged leaves.
A. dentata – 3 m. Yellow. June. Not as hardy as A. microphylla.

SITE & SOIL
3

PROPAGATION
1

FLOWER TIME
Depends on species

PRUNING
2   Late winter

BERBERIDOPSIS

Climber

B. corallina

B. corallina

Coral Plant

A twining or scrambling climber which provides a fine display of late summer flowers when grown in a mild area. A fussy plant, needing acid soil in a shady, sheltered spot.

VARIETIES Ⓔ

B. corallina – 3 m. Red. Long pendent clusters of flowers are borne at the tips of the stems. Each 1 cm bloom is carried on a long stalk. The oval and leathery leaves are dark green. Mulch around the stems in winter — new stems sprout after frost damage. The only species you are likely to find.

SITE & SOIL
14

PROPAGATION
1/6

FLOWER TIME
August — September

PRUNING
2   May

BERBERIS
Barberry

Shrub

Very popular flowering shrubs. There are tall spreading varieties and dwarf compact ones, deciduous types and evergreens — at the garden centre you will find plants for the rockery or border, for hedging or for covering bare ground. They all have a few features in common — the flowers are yellow or orange, they are prickly and all will thrive in almost any soil. They are not prone to insect attack, little or no pruning is required and there is no staking to worry about. Always buy a container-grown specimen.

B. darwinii

B. linearifolia

B. darwinii

VARIETIES	Ⓓ or Ⓔ

Evergreen types are grown for their flowers, berries and glossy leaves:
  B. darwinii – 2.5 m. Yellow. Reddish buds. Holly-like leaves.
  B. stenophylla – 2.5 m. Yellow.
  B. s. 'Corallina Compacta' – 30 cm. Yellow. Red buds.
  B. linearifolia – 2.5 m. Orange.
Deciduous types are grown for their berries and colourful leaves:
  B. thunbergii – 1.5 m. Red autumn leaves. Red berries.
  B. t. 'Atropurpurea' – 2 m. Bronzy red spring leaves.
  B. t. 'Harlequin' – 1.5 m. Cream-flecked leaves.
  B. t. 'Rose Glow' – 1.5 m. Pink-mottled leaves.

B. thunbergii 'Atropurpurea'

SITE & SOIL
10

PROPAGATION
1/6

B. stenophylla

FLOWER TIME
April — May

PRUNING
6

BETULA
Birch

Tree

B. pendula 'Youngii'

A popular tree with bark which is usually but not always white. Not difficult to grow but it is shallow-rooted — do not underplant and water during prolonged drought.

VARIETIES	Ⓓ

B. pendula – 9 m. Yellowish-green catkins. White, peeling bark. Pendulous branchlets.
B. p. 'Youngii' – 7 m. Pronounced weeping habit.
B. p. 'Purpurea' – 7 m. Purple leaves. Purple branches.
B. p. 'Fastigiata' – 5 m. Column-like.
B. albosinensis – 10 m. Red bark.

B. pendula

SITE & SOIL
10

PROPAGATION
5

FLOWER TIME
March — April

PRUNING
2   Early spring

14

BUDDLEIA
Butterfly Bush

Shrub

B. davidii
'Royal Red'

B. alternifolia

B. globosa

B. davidii 'Harlequin'

Buddleia is one of our favourite shrubs. The popular varieties are easy to grow but the display is often spoilt by neglect — failure to prune properly results in a gaunt bush with the flower-heads perched on bare branches. Buddleias have tapered leaves which are usually downy below and all bear clusters of tiny flowers which act as a magnet for butterflies. These blooms appear in late spring or late summer depending on the species. B alternifolia is the most attractive species when not in flower.

VARIETIES   Ⓓ or Ⓢ

B. davidii – 2.5 m if left unpruned. Various. Late July-mid September. Flower-heads are cone-shaped up to 40 cm long. Honey-scented. **'Royal Red'** (Purple-red), **'Ile de France'** (Violet), **'White Profusion'** (White), **'Empire Blue'** (Blue), **'Harlequin'** (Purple, variegated leaves).

B. 'Lochinch' – 2.5 m. Orange-eyed blue. July-August. Grey leaves.

B. alternifolia – 3 m. Lilac. June. Willow-like shrub. Arching stems.

B. globosa – 3 m. Orange. May-June. 4 cm wide ball-like flower-heads. Semi-evergreen.

B. fallowiana 'Alba' – 1.5 m. Orange-eyed white. July-August.

SITE & SOIL
2

PROPAGATION
1/3

B. alternifolia

FLOWER TIME
Depends on species

PRUNING
7

BUPLEURUM
B. fruticosum
Shrubby Hare's Ear

Shrub

B. fruticosum

It is hard to find, and for most gardeners it is not worth the trouble as the display is not particularly showy. Only two shrubby species are hardy enough for outdoors.

VARIETIES   Ⓔ

B. fruticosum – 1.5 m. Yellow. Tiny flowers are borne in 10 cm wide circular heads. Leathery glossy leaves are greyish-green above, silvery below. Seed-heads remain over winter. Good for seaside gardens — thrives in sandy soil and salt-laden air.

B. angulosum – 3 m. Pale green.

SITE & SOIL
3

PROPAGATION
1

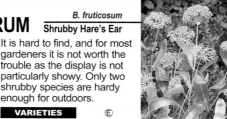

FLOWER TIME
July — September

PRUNING	
2	Spring

BUXUS

Shrub

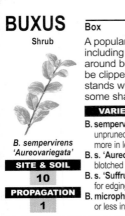

B. sempervirens
'Aureovariegata'

SITE & SOIL
10

PROPAGATION
1

B. sempervirens

Box

A popular choice for hedging, including dwarf hedging around beds. The stems can be clipped regularly. Withstands wind, alkaline soil and some shade.

VARIETIES   Ⓔ

B. sempervirens – 3 m if left unpruned. Oval leaves 2.5 cm or more in length.

B. s. 'Aureovariegata' – Yellow-blotched leaves.

B. s. 'Suffruticosa' – Dwarf variety for edging beds.

B. microphylla – Oval leaves 2 cm or less in length.

FLOWER TIME
—

PRUNING
2

CALLICARPA

Shrub

C. bodinieri giraldii 'Profusion'

SITE & SOIL
2

PROPAGATION
1/6

C. bodinieri giraldii 'Profusion'

Beauty Berry

In autumn the leaves turn red or violet, and when they fall the polished berries are revealed on the bare stems — the berry clusters persist until Christmas. Plant in groups.

VARIETIES   Ⓓ

C. bodinieri giraldii 'Profusion' – 2 m. Pale pink. August. Flowers are insignificant — it is grown for its pale purple berries. Needs shelter. Most popular variety.

C. japonica 'Leucocarpa' – 1 m. Pink. Violet berries.

C. dichotoma – 1.2 m. Pink. Lilac berries.

BERRY TIME
September — December

PRUNING
2

CALLISTEMON

Shrub

C. citrinus 'Splendens'

SITE & SOIL
9

PROPAGATION
1

C. rigidus

Bottle Brush

Small blooms with prominent stamens are tightly packed along a cylindrical spike. The popular species are reasonably hardy, but grow against a sunny wall.

VARIETIES   Ⓔ

C. citrinus 'Splendens' – 2 m. Red. Bottle brush flower-heads 5 cm long. Narrow 4 cm long leaves which emit a lemon aroma when crushed.

C. rigidus – 1.5 m. Red. Hardier than variety above.

C. sieberi – 1 m. Creamy-yellow.

C. linearis – 2.5 m. Greenish-red.

FLOWER TIME
June — July

PRUNING
2

CALLUNA

Shrub

The popular heathers grown in the garden are varieties of either Calluna or Erica. It is easy to confuse the two, but there are several basic differences. There are no mid winter- or spring-flowering varieties of Calluna and none of them can tolerate lime. With most Callunas the showy part of the flower is the calyx and not the petals, and coloured foliage (red, gold, bronze, grey etc) is much more common than with Ericas. Some green-leaved ones change colour in autumn. All relish starved soil and sunshine.

C. vulgaris 'Beoley Gold'

C. vulgaris 'Gold Haze'

VARIETIES   Ⓔ

C. vulgaris is the only species, but there are many varieties:

C. v. 'Gold Haze' – 45 cm. White. August-September. Yellow leaves.

C. v. 'Beoley Gold' – 40 cm. White. August-September. Gold leaves.

C. v. 'Blazeaway' – 45 cm. Lilac. August-September. Red in winter.

C. v. 'Peter Sparkes' – 40 cm. Pink. Double. September-October.

C. v. 'Tib' – 30 cm. Rose-pink. July-August.

C. v. 'H.E. Beale' – 45 cm. Pink. Double. September-October.

C. v. 'Kinlochruel' – 25 cm. Pink. Double. September-October.

C. v. 'County Wicklow' – 25 cm. Pink. Double. August-October.

C. vulgaris 'H.E. Beale'

SITE & SOIL
9

PROPAGATION
1/6

C. vulgaris 'Peter Sparkes'

FLOWER TIME
Depends on variety

PRUNING	
10	March

CALOCEDRUS

C. decurrens
Incense Cedar

Conifer

Tiny scale-like leaves with outward-spreading tips emit an incense-like aroma when crushed. Cones appear at the tips of drooping shoots. May be listed as Libocedrus.

VARIETIES   Ⓔ

C. decurrens – 1.8 m; 18 m when mature. The only species you are likely to find. Broadly conical at first, becoming columnar with age. Remains clothed with leafy branches down to ground level.

C. d. 'Aureovariegata' – Slower growing than the species. Gold-splashed leaves.

C. decurrens

SITE & SOIL
4

PROPAGATION
5

FLOWER TIME
—

PRUNING
1

CALYCANTHUS

C. floridus
Allspice

Shrub

C. occidentalis

Despite its attractive features this American shrub is not easy to find. It is hardy, the many-petalled blooms are large and all parts are aromatic.

VARIETIES ⓓ

C. floridus – 2 m. Reddish-brown. 5 cm wide flowers have strap-like petals and sepals. Large oval leaves. Easy to grow, but a few branches may die back in winter if the site is exposed.
C. f. 'Purpureus' – Leaves purplish below. Rare.
C. occidentalis – 2 m. Deep red.

SITE & SOIL
3

PROPAGATION
1/6

FLOWER TIME
June — July

PRUNING
2   Spring

CAMELLIA

Camellia

Shrub

C. japonica
'Adolphe Audusson'

C. williamsii
'J.C. Williams'

C. 'Leonard Messel'

One of the most attractive of all shrubs in the right situation. The glossy oval leaves are present all year round and the showy 5-15 cm blooms are available in a wide range of white, pinks and reds. These flowers are sometimes single, but the semi-double and double varieties are more popular. Camellias are hardy and provide a fine spring display, but they are not for everyone. Non-alkaline soil is essential, and they are not suitable for sites which are exposed to cold winds or the early morning sun.

C. japonica 'Lavinia Magg

VARIETIES ⓔ

C. japonica – 2 m. Various. February-April. Faded blooms remain on branches.
C. j. 'Adolphe Audusson' – Red. Semi-double.
C. j. 'Elegans' – Peach-pink. Anemone-shaped.
C. j. 'Lavinia Maggi' – Rose-striped white. Double.
C. williamsii – 2 m. Various. February-May. Freer flowering than above. Faded blooms fall naturally.
C. w. 'Donation' – Pink. Semi-double.
C. w. 'J.C. Williams' – Pink. Single.
C. w. 'Saint Ewe' – Pink. Single.
C. 'Leonard Messel' – Pink. Semi-double.

C. williamsii 'Donation'

SITE & SOIL
6

PROPAGATION
1

FLOWER TIME
Depends on species

PRUNING
2   May

CAMPSIS

C. grandiflora

Trumpet Vine

Climber

C. radicans

This self-clinging climber is grown for its trumpet-like flowers which are borne in clusters. Provide shelter, support and as much sun as possible.

VARIETIES Ⓓ

C. grandiflora – 6 m. Red/orange. Flowers 5-8 cm long.

C. radicans – 5 m. Red/orange. Hardier than C. grandiflora.

C. r. 'Flava' – 5 m. Yellow. Yellow Trumpet Vine.

C. tagliabuana 'Madame Galen' – 5 m. Reddish salmon. Hybrid of the 2 species — hardier than both.

SITE & SOIL
1

PROPAGATION
1/6

FLOWER TIME
August — September

PRUNING
9   March

CARAGANA

C. arborescens

Pea Tree

Shrub
•
Tree

C. arborescens

A shrub or weeping tree which will thrive in starved soil and windswept locations. Not popular — the problem is that the flowers are small and not particularly numerous.

VARIETIES Ⓓ

C. arborescens – 4 m. Yellow. Fragrant flowers borne in clusters. Fast-growing shrub or tree.

C. a. 'Lorbergii' – 4 m. Yellow. Thread-like leaves.

C. a. 'Pendula' – Yellow. 1.5 m or 2.5 m as a weeping standard.

C. a. 'Walker' – Yellow. 1 m or 2 m as a weeping standard.

SITE & SOIL
10

PROPAGATION
1

FLOWER TIME
May

PRUNING
1

CARPENTERIA

C. californica

Tree Anemone

Shrub

C. californica

A beautiful but unusual shrub which needs the protection of a south- or west-facing wall. Some shoots may be killed if winter frosts are prolonged. Flowers are large and fragrant.

VARIETIES Ⓔ

C. californica – 2 m. White. Flowers bear a central boss of golden stamens. Lance-shaped leaves — glossy green above, woolly white below. If possible buy a container-grown specimen when in flower.

C. c. 'Ladham's Variety' – 2 m. White. Freer-flowering than the species — blooms 8 cm across.

SITE & SOIL
1

PROPAGATION
1

FLOWER TIME
June — July

PRUNING
2   Spring

CARPINUS

Hornbeam

Tree

Hornbeam is a stately tree, but it has none of the popularity of its taller relative, the Common Beech. Like beech it keeps its leaves over winter when used for hedging.

VARIETIES   Ⓓ

C. betulus – 8 m; 15 m when mature. Common Hornbeam. Unlike beech the leaves are saw-edged and the fruits are hop-like. The grey, fluted bark is attractive. Use for hedging or as a specimen tree. Not fussy about soil type.

C. betulus

SITE & SOIL
10

PROPAGATION
7

C. b. 'Fastigiata' – 7 m; 12 m when mature. Upright growth.

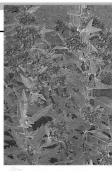

FLOWER TIME
—

PRUNING	
2	Spring

CARYOPTERIS

C. clandonensis 'Kew Blue'

Blue Spiraea

Shrub

A rounded shrub for the front of the border — plant several in a group. It will thrive in all sorts of soils including chalky ones. Not as frost-sensitive as once thought.

VARIETIES   Ⓓ

C. clandonensis – 1 m. Lavender. 10 cm long terminal clusters of small fluffy flowers. Grey-green leaves.

C. clandonensis

SITE & SOIL
1

PROPAGATION
1

C. c. 'Arthur Simmonds' – Blue.
C. c. 'Kew Blue' – Dark blue.
C. c. 'Worcester Gold' – Blue. Young foliage is golden.
C. incana – 1.2 m. Pale blue.

FLOWER TIME
September — October

PRUNING	
11	March

CASSINIA

C. fulvida

Cassinia

Shrub

Cassinia can be used to add height to a heather bed as it grows to over 1 m. The foliage is yellow, green or grey and in summer flat heads of tiny white flowers appear.

VARIETIES   Ⓔ

C. fulvida – 1.2 m. White. Flower-heads bear tiny daisy-like blooms. 1 cm long leaves cover the stems — pale yellow in spring darkening to orange in autumn.

C. vauvilliersii

SITE & SOIL
9

PROPAGATION
1

C. vauvilliersii – 1.5 m. White. Dark green leaves.
C. v. 'Albida' – Mealy white coating over stems and leaves.

FLOWER TIME
July — August

PRUNING	
2	March

CASSIOPE

Cassiope

C. 'Muirhead'

Shrub

C. 'Edinburgh'

Unlike Calluna and Erica this heather-like plant has scale-like leaves which clasp the stem to give a whipcord effect. A useful addition if the site is acidic and sunny.

VARIETIES   Ⓔ

C. mertensiana – 20 cm. Creamy white. Bell-like flowers have red or green sepals.
C. 'Muirhead' – 25 cm. White. Dark green leaves.
C. 'Edinburgh' – 25 cm. Brown sepals.
C. tetragona – 25 cm. Red sepals.
C. lycopodioides – 8 cm. White.

SITE & SOIL
14

PROPAGATION
1

FLOWER TIME
April — May

PRUNING
2   Early spring

CASTANEA

Sweet Chestnut

C. sativa

Tree

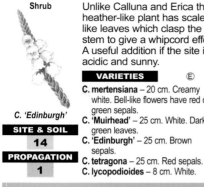

C. sativa

A tree noted for its drought resistance, long life and an autumn crop of edible nuts after a hot dry summer. It is a plant for parkland rather than your plot.

VARIETIES   Ⓓ

C. sativa – 14 m. Pale yellow cat-kins. Shiny leaves. Bark of mature tree has deep spiral grooves. Brown chestnuts form within round, prickly fruit-case.
C. s. 'Albomarginata' – White-edged leaves.
C. s. 'Variegata' – Yellow-edged leaves.

SITE & SOIL
10

PROPAGATION
7

FLOWER TIME
July

PRUNING
2   Early spring

CATALPA

Indian Bean Tree

C. bignonioides

Tree
•
Shrub

C. bignonioides

This summer-flowering tree or shrub is easily recognised by its unusually large heart-shaped leaves. Quick-growing and wide-spreading — well-suited to town gardens.

VARIETIES   Ⓓ

C. bignonioides – 9 m; 12 m when mature. Yellow- and purple-flecked white. Flowers are Horse Chestnut-like — followed by long thin pods. Boughs may break in strong wind. Not good on heavy soil.
C. b. 'Aurea' – 3 m. White. Yellow leaves. Less hardy than the species. Grow it as a shrub.

SITE & SOIL
4

PROPAGATION
5

FLOWER TIME
August

PRUNING
2   Early spring

CEANOTHUS

C. thyrsiflorus 'Repens'
Evergreen Californian Lilac

Shrub

Most varieties belong here. In general they are the less hardy ones — grow against a warm wall. The leaves are small and glossy and the flowers are in thimble-like clusters.

C. 'Burkwoodii'

VARIETIES Ⓔ

C. thyrsiflorus 'Repens' – 80 cm. Blue. May-June.
C. 'Blue Mound' – 1 m. Dark blue. May-June.
C. 'Burkwoodii' – 2 m. Blue. May and September.
C. 'Autumnal Blue' – 2.5 m. Blue. July-September.
C. 'Trewithen Blue' – 4 m. Tender.

SITE & SOIL
1

PROPAGATION
1

FLOWER TIME
Depends on species

PRUNING
10 After flowering

CEANOTHUS

C. pallidus 'Perle Rose'
Deciduous Californian Lilac

Shrub

This group are hardier than the evergreens. The leaves are larger and the flower clusters are bigger and looser. Plant in spring — do not grow in chalky soil.

C. 'Gloire de Versailles'

VARIETIES Ⓓ

C. 'Gloire de Versailles' – 2 m. Sky blue. Large clusters. Popular.
C. 'Topaz' – 1.5 m. Blue — darker than 'Gloire de Versailles'.
C. 'Henri Desfosse' – 1.5 m. Dark blue.
C. pallidus 'Marie Simon' – 1.5 m. Pale pink. Upright growth.
C. p. 'Perle Rose' – 1.5 m. Pink.

SITE & SOIL
1

PROPAGATION
1

FLOWER TIME
July — October

PRUNING
9 March

CEDRUS

C. deodara 'Golden Horizon'
Cedar

Conifer

The basic species are too large for the ordinary garden, but there are dwarf varieties and slow-growing weeping types. Needles are arranged in tufts.

C. libani

VARIETIES Ⓔ

C. libani – 2 m; 25 m when mature. Cedar of Lebanon. Smaller varieties include **'Nana'** and **'Sargentii'**.
C. atlantica 'Glauca' – 3 m. Blue-green leaves. Blue Cedar. Smaller varieties include **'Glauca Pendula'**.
C. deodara – 3 m. Drooping growth habit. Smaller varieties include **'Aurea'** and **'Golden Horizon'**.

SITE & SOIL
2

PROPAGATION
5

FLOWER TIME
—

PRUNING
1

CELASTRUS

C. orbiculatus
Bittersweet

Climber

In summer there is nothing special about this climber — insignificant flowers appear in July. In autumn its coloured leaves and fruits make it an eye-catching plant.

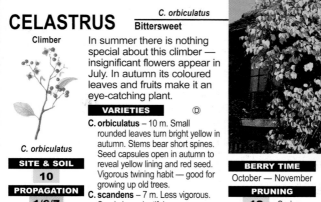

C. orbiculatus

VARIETIES · Ⓓ

C. orbiculatus – 10 m. Small rounded leaves turn bright yellow in autumn. Stems bear short spines. Seed capsules open in autumn to reveal yellow lining and red seed. Vigorous twining habit — good for growing up old trees.

C. scandens – 7 m. Less vigorous. Seeds less plentiful.

SITE & SOIL
10

PROPAGATION
1/6/7

BERRY TIME
October — November

PRUNING
12 · Spring

CEPHALOTAXUS

C. harringtonia 'Fastigiata'
Plum Yew

Conifer

A neat shrub which can be hard pruned to provide a hedge or screen. Other advantages include the ability to flourish in shade and to grow in alkaline soil.

C. harringtonia 'Drupacea'

VARIETIES · Ⓔ

C. harringtonia 'Drupacea' – 3 m. 4 cm long strap-like leaves give it yew-like appearance. The cones, however, are different — the 2.5 cm long fruits are olive-like.

C. h. 'Fastigiata' – 5 m. Differs from the above variety by its upright growth and near-black leaves spirally arranged around stem.

SITE & SOIL
15

PROPAGATION
5

FLOWER TIME
—

PRUNING
13 · Early summer

CERATOSTIGMA

C. willmottianum
Hardy Plumbago

Shrub

The stems of this low-growing shrub may be killed by frost, but hard pruning in spring will ensure new stems which bear clusters of phlox-like flowers in summer and autumn.

C. willmottianum

VARIETIES · Ⓓ

C. willmottianum – 1 m. Blue. Foliage turns red in autumn. The hardiest species.

C. griffithii – 1 m. Blue. Leaves broader and flowers darker than C. willmottianum — less hardy.

C. plumbaginoides – 50 cm. Blue. Low-growing, can be used as ground cover.

SITE & SOIL
1

PROPAGATION
1/10

FLOWER TIME
July — October

PRUNING
11 · April

CERCIS

C. siliquastrum

Shrub
•
Tree

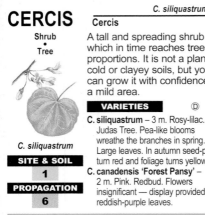

C. siliquastrum

Cercis

A tall and spreading shrub which in time reaches tree-like proportions. It is not a plant for cold or clayey soils, but you can grow it with confidence in a mild area.

VARIETIES ⒟

C. siliquastrum – 3 m. Rosy-lilac. Judas Tree. Pea-like blooms wreathe the branches in spring. Large leaves. In autumn seed-pods turn red and foliage turns yellow.
C. canadensis 'Forest Pansy' – 2 m. Pink. Redbud. Flowers insignificant — display provided by reddish-purple leaves.

SITE & SOIL
1

PROPAGATION
6

FLOWER TIME
May — June

PRUNING	
2	Early spring

CHAENOMELES   Japonica

Shrub

C. speciosa

C. speciosa 'Nivalis'

An old favourite which you will find in gardens everywhere. The Latin name is Chaenomeles, but it is better known as Japonica, Cydonia or Ornamental Quince. There are several reasons for its popularity — it thrives in all types of soil, it flourishes in both sun and shade, and its bright spring flowers are followed by large golden fruits which are edible, but taste-less. Grow it as a 1-2 m bush or plant it against a wall where it may reach 3 m or more. It can also be grown as an informal hedge.

VARIETIES ⒟

C. speciosa – 2-3 m. Various. Tall — varieties are good wall plants. Leaves rather sparse.
C. s. 'Nivalis' – White. Vigorous.
C. s. 'Moerloosei' – Pink/white.
C. s. 'Geisha Girl' – Pink/yellow.
C. s. 'Simonii' – Red. Low-growing.
C. superba – 1.2 m. Various. Dense, rounded bush — varieties are good border plants.
C. s. 'Knap Hill Scarlet' – Orange-red.
C. s. 'Crimson & Gold' – Red petals, golden anthers.
C. s. 'Pink Lady' – Pink. Red buds.
C. s. 'Nicoline' – Red.
C. japonica – 1 m. Orange-red. Late flowering. Suckers freely.

SITE & SOIL
16

PROPAGATION
1

C. superba 'Crimson & Gold'

C. superba 'Knap Hill Scarlet'

FLOWER TIME
March — May

PRUNING	
13	After flowering

CHAMAECYPARIS False Cypress

Conifer

C. lawsoniana

You will have no difficulty in finding specimens — even a modest garden centre will offer several varieties and you will find scores listed by specialist nurseries. Choose with care — there are dwarfs for the rockery and tall trees for the large garden. It is closely related to Cupressus, but the branches are flat and not rounded sprays, and the cones are only 3-4 cm across. It is also hardier and easier to transplant, but it is not a grow-anywhere plant. Chamae-cyparis can fail in a poorly-drained and exposed site.

C. lawsoniana 'Minima Aurea'

VARIETIES   Ⓔ

C. lawsoniana – The most popular species:
C. l. 'Elwoodii' – 1.5 m. Dense, conical shrub. Grey-green, turns steely blue in winter.
C. l. 'Elwood's Gold' – 1 m. Gold-tipped green.
C. l. 'Columnaris' – 2 m; 8 m when mature. Blue-grey. Column-shaped.
C. l. 'Pembury Blue' – 3 m; 15 m when mature. Blue-grey.
C. l. 'Lane' – 2 m. Gold. Column-shaped.
C. l. 'Minima Aurea' – 30 cm. Yellow.
C. l. 'Pygmaea Argentea' – 30 cm. Silver-tipped blue-green.
C. nootkatensis 'Pendula' – 2.5 m. One of the most pendulous of all tall conifers.
C. obtusa 'Nana Gracilis' – 50 cm; 3 m when mature. Shell-shaped sprays of branchlets.
C. pisifera 'Boulevard' – 1 m; 3 m when mature. Silvery blue. Feathery leaves. Neat conical shrub. Popular.

C. pisifera 'Boulevard'

SITE & SOIL	PROPAGATION
2	5

FLOWER TIME	PRUNING
—	14

CHIMONANTHUS Winter Sweet

Shrub

C. praecox

C. praecox 'Luteus'

The flowers on the bare stems are not particularly eye-catching, but they do appear early and have a spicy aroma. Flowers may take several years to appear.

VARIETIES   Ⓓ

C. praecox – 2 m; 3 m when grown against a wall. Purple-centred pale yellow. December-March. Pendent blooms have waxy petals.
C. p. 'Grandiflorus' – Red-centred yellow. December-March. Less fragrant than the species.
C. p. 'Luteus' – Yellow. February-March. Showier than C. praecox.

SITE & SOIL	PROPAGATION
2	6

FLOWER TIME	
Depends on species	

PRUNING	
2	After flowering

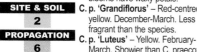

CHOISYA

C. ternata 'Sundance'

Mexican Orange Blossom

Shrub

This neat and rounded shrub provides year-round dense leaf cover. Flat heads of waxy flowers appear in spring — both leaves and flowers have an orange-like fragrance.

C. ternata

VARIETIES ⒠

C. ternata – 2.5 m. White. Oval dark green leaflets. Frost damage likely on exposed sites. Late summer flowers occasionally appear.

C. t. 'Sundance' – 1 m. White. Grown for its yellow leaves, but rarely flowers. Rather tender.

C. 'Aztec Pearl' – 2 m. White. Narrow leaflets. Not scented.

SITE & SOIL
3

PROPAGATION
1

FLOWER TIME
April — May

PRUNING	
8	After flowering

CISTUS

Rock Rose

Shrub

C. 'Silver Pink'

C. cyprius

C. purpureus

The flowers look like single roses with petals which are often blotched at the base. These blooms are short-lived — the papery petals open in the morning and drop before nightfall, but new buds appear regularly and the shrub is constantly in bloom during the summer months. This rounded evergreen is a good choice for borders and rockeries but it is not happy in clay or shade. Heavy frosts are a problem — no variety is completely hardy. Do not confuse with the Sun Rose Helianthemum.

VARIETIES ⒠

Short varieties (1 m or less):
C. corbariensis – White.
C. 'Silver Pink' – Silvery pink.
C. dansereaui 'Decumbens' – Maroon-blotched white.
C. skanbergii – Pink.
C. pulverulentus 'Sunset' – Pink.
Tall varieties (over 1 m) — usually less hardy than short varieties:
C. cyprius – 1.8 m. Maroon-blotched white.
C. purpureus – 1.2 m. Maroon-blotched pink.
C. laurifolius – 1.5 m. White.
Halimium varieties — closely related and similar to Cistus:
Halimium lasianthum – 1 m. Yellow.

C. pulverulentus 'Sunset'

Halimium lasianthum

SITE & SOIL
1

PROPAGATION
1

FLOWER TIME
June — August

PRUNING	
2	Spring

CLEMATIS

Virgin's Bower

Climber

C. 'Nelly Moser'

C. 'The President'

C. montana

Clematis is our most popular climber but it is not an easy plant. If you have several varieties then you will have to learn something about their classification and needs. There are two basic types. The Species group bloom in spring, have smaller flowers and are easier to grow. The Large-flowered Hybrids are showier and, depending on the variety, flower between May and October. The soil around roots should be in shade and the stem in the sun. Set stem/root junction 3 cm below soil level.

VARIETIES   Ⓓ or ⓈⒺ or Ⓔ

Large-flowered Hybrid group – 3 m. Various. 10-20 cm wide blooms.
  C. 'Nelly Moser' – Pink-tinged white, striped red. May & August.
  C. 'The President' – Purple, silver reverse. June-September.
  C. 'Jackmanii Superba' – Violet-purple. July-September.
  C. 'Ville de Lyon' – Red, darker edge. July-October.
Species group – 10 m. Various.
  C. montana – White. May.
  C. macropetala – White, blue or pink. May-June. Pendent flowers.
  C. alpina – Various. April-May.
  C. tangutica – Yellow. August.
  C. armandii – White. April. Evergreen.

C. 'Ville de Lyon'

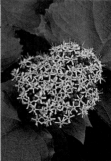

C. macropetala

FLOWER TIME
Depends on variety

PRUNING
15

CLERODENDRUM

C. bungei
Glory Tree

Shrub

C. trichotomum

SITE & SOIL
3

PROPAGATION
8

There is an interesting contrast in smells — the flowers have a pleasant fragrance but bruised leaves emit a distinctly unpleasant odour. Choose a sheltered spot.

VARIETIES   Ⓓ

C. trichotomum – 3 m. White. Leaves purple when young. Shrub becomes tree-like with age. Pinkish buds open into starry flowers — in autumn each one becomes a blue berry within a red calyx.
C. bungei – 2 m. Rose-red. Ball-like flower-heads. Frost damages shoots.

FLOWER TIME
August — September

PRUNING
2   Spring

27

CLETHRA

C. alnifolia 'Paniculata'
Summersweet

Shrub

The small summer flowers are clustered in long terminal spikes. These bottle brush flower-heads are fragrant and the autumn foliage may be attractively coloured.

C. alnifolia

VARIETIES ⓓ

C. alnifolia – 2 m. White. Flower-heads 12 cm long.
C. a. 'Paniculata' – Larger flowers.
C. a. 'Rosea' – Pale pink.
C. a. 'Pink Spire' – Pink.
C. barbinervis – 3 m. White. Red/yellow leaves in autumn.
C. delavayi – 4 m. White. Pendent flowers.

SITE & SOIL
14

PROPAGATION
8

FLOWER TIME
July — August

PRUNING
2   Early spring

COLUTEA

C. arborescens
Bladder Senna

Shrub

The pea-like flowers, though small, appear throughout the summer and autumn. The inflated seed pods pop when pressed, but remember the seeds are poisonous.

C. arborescens

VARIETIES ⓓ

C. arborescens – 2.5 m. Yellow. Leaves made up of paired leaflets. Pale brown 8 cm long seed pods. Vigorous much-branched growth habit.
C. media – 2 m. Bronze. Grey-green leaves.
C. m. 'Copper Beauty' – 2 m. Coppery red. Grey-green leaves.

SITE & SOIL
11

PROPAGATION
1

FLOWER TIME
June — October

PRUNING
8   Late spring

CONVOLVULUS

C. cneorum
Shrubby Bindweed

Shrub

An attractive but rather tender shrub. The leaves are silvery-grey and the flowers appear throughout the summer months — a plant for year-round interest.

C. cneorum

VARIETIES ⓔ

C. cneorum – 50 cm. White, striped with pink on reverse. Pink buds open into 4 cm wide trumpet-shaped blooms. 3 cm long leaves covered with silky hairs. Spreads to about 80 cm — use it to provide ground cover or grow in a container. Frost may damage the foliage — plant in a sheltered spot.

SITE & SOIL
1

PROPAGATION
1

FLOWER TIME
May — August

PRUNING
13   Early spring

CORDYLINE

C. australis 'Torbay Dazzler'
Cabbage Palm

Tree

C. australis

This palm-like plant is usually bought as a rosette of arching leaves — in time it becomes a short tree. Grow it in a large pot or in a sunny border in a mild locality.

VARIETIES ⒠

C. australis – 2 m. White. Large head of tiny blooms after a few years. Pale green 30 cm-1 m long leaves. Choose a sheltered spot.
C. a. 'Purpurea' – Purple leaves.
C. a. 'Torbay Dazzler' – White-striped green leaves.
C. a. 'Albertii' – Red/pink/cream/green leaves.

SITE & SOIL
4

PROPAGATION
8

FLOWER TIME
June

PRUNING
16 Spring

CORNUS

C. alba 'Sibirica'
Coloured-bark Dogwood

Shrub

C. alba

The coloured-bark dogwoods form bright thickets of eye-catching stems in winter. All are easy to grow and some bear variegated leaves. Hard pruning is necessary.

VARIETIES ⒟

C. alba – 2 m. White. Red stems. Clusters of small flowers.
C. a. 'Sibirica' – Bright red stems.
C. a. 'Elegantissima' – White-edged leaves.
C. a. 'Spaethii' – Yellow-edged leaves.
C. stolonifera 'Flaviramea' – 2 m. White. Yellow stems.

SITE & SOIL
10

PROPAGATION
3

FLOWER TIME
June

PRUNING
11 Early spring

CORNUS

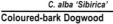
C. mas
Flowering Dogwood

Shrub
•
Tree

C. florida 'Rubra'

The flowers are often bold and the autumn leaves are brightly coloured. Some grow tall with architectural tree-like shapes and one is a ground cover. Should be more popular.

VARIETIES ⒟

C. florida 'Rubra' – 3 m. Rose-red. June-July. Red leaves in autumn.
C. kousa 'Chinensis' – 3 m. White. May-June. 8 cm wide blooms.
C. controversa – 1.5 m. White. June. Tiered branches.
C. mas – 3 m. Yellow. February.
C. canadensis – 20 cm. White. June-July.

SITE & SOIL
9

PROPAGATION
1

FLOWER TIME
Depends on species

PRUNING
2 Spring

CORONILLA

C. valentina
'Glauca Variegata'
Coronilla

Shrub

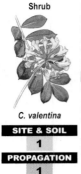

C. valentina

Reasonably reliable when grown against a sunny wall. Its outstanding feature is that it starts to flower in spring and then continues at intervals until the first frosts.

VARIETIES Ⓓ or Ⓔ

C. valentina – 1.5 m. Yellow. Pea-like flowers 1.5 cm long.
C. v. 'Glauca' – 1 m. Yellow.
C. v. 'Glauca Variegata' – Cream-splashed leaves.
C. v. 'Glauca Citrina' – Pale yellow.
Hippocrepis emerus – 2.5 m. Yellow. Deciduous. Sometimes listed as **C. emerus**.

SITE & SOIL
1

PROPAGATION
1

FLOWER TIME
May — October

PRUNING
8 Spring

CORYLOPSIS

C. pauciflora
Winter Hazel

Shrub

C. spicata

Tassels of flowers appear before the leaves. Not as popular as its relative Witch Hazel — the problem is that it is not robust and frost can damage the blooms.

VARIETIES Ⓓ

C. pauciflora – 1.2 m. Yellow. Leaves pink when young.
C. spicata – 2 m. Yellow. Purple-anthered flowers.
C. glabrescens – 3.5 m. Yellow. Free-flowering. Wide-spreading.
C. willmottiae 'Spring Purple' – 2 m. Yellow. Leaves purple when young.

SITE & SOIL
6

PROPAGATION
1

FLOWER TIME
March — April

PRUNING
2 After flowering

CORYLUS

C. avellana 'Contorta'
Hazel

Shrub
•
Tree
C. avellana 'Contorta'

C. maxima 'Purpurea'

Green-leaved types are used for hedging, but there are colourful ones to grow as specimen plants. Winter catkins hang from the bare branches.

VARIETIES Ⓓ

C. avellana – 3 m. Yellow. Yellow leaves in autumn.
C. a. 'Aurea' – 2 m. Yellow. Golden Nut. Yellow leaves.
C. a. 'Contorta' – 3 m. Yellow. Corkscrew Hazel. Twisted stems.
C. maxima 'Purpurea' – 2.5 m. Purple. Purple leaves and nuts.
C. colurna – 10 m. Stately tree.

SITE & SOIL
4

PROPAGATION
8

FLOWER TIME
February

PRUNING
8 March

COTINUS

C. coggygria
'Notcutt's Variety'

Smoke Bush

Shrub
•
Tree

C. coggygria

Easy to recognise. Intricately-branched flower-heads appear in summer and after flowering the feathery stalks remain. They give a smoke-like effect, hence the common name.

VARIETIES   Ⓓ

C. coggygria – 3 m. Pink. Old name **Rhus cotinus**. Flower stalks turn grey with age. Yellow leaves in autumn.

C. c. 'Notcutt's Variety' – 3 m. Purple-pink. Red leaves.

C. c. 'Royal Purple' – 3 m. Purple-pink. Purple leaves.

C. 'Grace' – 4 m. Purple leaves.

SITE & SOIL
2

PROPAGATION
8

FLOWER TIME
June

PRUNING	
2	Spring

COTONEASTER   Cotoneaster

Shrub

C. 'Cornubia'

C. 'Cornubia'

One of the most important and useful berrying shrubs in the garden. They come in all sorts of shapes and sizes, and most of the species are evergreen or semi-evergreen. Unlike Pyracantha the oval leaves are smooth-edged and the branches are thornless. Pink buds open in May or June into white flowers and in autumn there is a display of showy berries which birds do not find particularly attractive. With some varieties there is a bold show of bright autumn leaf colours. Cut back shrubs if they get out of hand.

C. dammeri

VARIETIES   Ⓓ or ⓈⒺ or Ⓔ

Evergreen group:

C. dammeri – 20 cm. Red berries. Prostrate. Wide-spreading. Popular.

C. 'Gnom' – 30 cm. Red berries. Good ground cover. Few berries.

C. 'Coral Beauty' – 1 m. Orange berries. Semi-prostrate.

C. conspicuus 'Decorus' – 1 m. Red berries. Arching branches.

C. 'Cornubia' – 3 m. Grow as a standard. Abundant berries.

C. lacteus – 3 m. Red berries. Large leaves. Good hedging plant.

Deciduous group:

C. horizontalis – 50 cm. Red berries. Fan-like branches. Popular.

C. h. 'Variegatus' – 50 cm. Red berries. White-edged leaves.

C. horizontalis

C. horizontalis

SITE & SOIL
10

PROPAGATION
1

BERRY TIME
October — January

PRUNING	
2	Spring

CRATAEGUS   Hawthorn

Tree
•
Shrub

C. monogyna

C. prunifolia

C. orientalis

A familiar sight in the garden as a small tree, large shrub or hedge. Over the years it has acquired many names — May, Quickthorn, Hawthorn etc. The thorny branches bear clusters of white, pink or red flowers in late spring or early summer and these are followed by red or orange berries in autumn. The leaves may turn red or orange at the end of the season. One of the great virtues of Crataegus is that it will grow almost anywhere once it is established, in dry or poorly-drained soil and in sun or shade.

C. monogyna

VARIETIES   Ⓓ

C. monogyna – 6 m. White. Common Hawthorn. Red berries.
C. m. 'Stricta' – 5 m. Column-shaped.
C. laevigata – 5 m. Varieties are popular — leaves less deeply lobed, stems less spiny and growth less vigorous than C. monogyna:
C. l. 'Paul's Scarlet' – Red. Double.
C. l. 'Plena' – White. Double.
C. l. 'Rosea Flore Pleno' – Pink. Double.
C. orientalis – 5 m. White. Large orange-red berries.
C. lavallei – 7 m. White. Orange berries. Few thorns.
C. prunifolia – 5 m. White. Showy red berries. Red leaves in autumn.

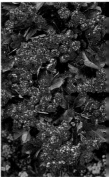

C. laevigata 'Paul's Scarle[t]

| SITE & SOIL | 16 |
| PROPAGATION | 5 |

| FLOWER TIME |
| May — June |
| PRUNING |
| 2   Late winter |

CRINODENDRON

C. hookerianum
Lantern Tree

Shrub

C. hookerianum

The fleshy-petalled flowers hang down from the branches on long stalks. Despite their appeal it is not a popular plant — a mild and sheltered site is required.

VARIETIES   Ⓔ

C. hookerianum – 2.5 m. Red. Lantern-like flowers. Buds appear in winter, swell in spring and open fully in early summer. Lance-shaped 5 cm long leaves.
C. patagua – 3.5 m. White. Quite different to C. hookerianum — the bell-shaped, fringed flowers do not open until late summer.

| SITE & SOIL | 14 |
| PROPAGATION | 1 |

| FLOWER TIME |
| Depends on species |
| PRUNING |
| 2   Spring |

CRYPTOMERIA

Japanese Cedar

Conifer

Cryptomeria japonica is a tall tree which has no place in the average garden. There are, however, several dwarf varieties. Green leaves change to reddish-bronze in winter.

VARIETIES Ⓔ

C. japonica – 25 m when mature. Juvenile leaves feathery — mature leaves short and awl-shaped.
C. j. 'Elegans' – 3 m. Feathery — adult leaves do not appear.
C. j. 'Nana' – 2 m. Compact, slow-growing. Curved branchlet tips.
C. j. 'Vilmoriniana' – 1 m. Ball-shaped. Popular rockery conifer.

C. japonica

SITE & SOIL
9

PROPAGATION
5

FLOWER TIME
—

PRUNING
1

CUNNINGHAMIA

C. lanceolata

Chinese Fir

Conifer

When young it forms a pyramid of branches densely clothed with shiny leaves, giving it a Monkey Puzzle Tree appearance. Requires protection from strong winds.

VARIETIES Ⓔ

C. lanceolata – 2.5 m. Narrow 5 cm long leaves are arranged spirally around the branches — each one marked below with two white bands. Attractive when young, but becomes gaunt and unattractive with age. Leaves turn brown in autumn. Round 4 cm cones have sharply-pointed scales.

C. lanceolata

SITE & SOIL
9

PROPAGATION
5

FLOWER TIME
—

PRUNING
1

CUPRESSOCYPARIS

C. leylandii 'Castlewellan'

Leyland Cypress

Conifer

'Leylandii' has replaced Lawson Cypress (page 25) as our most popular conifer hedge — it withstands hard pruning. Warning — it can be a menace if neglected.

VARIETIES Ⓔ

C. leylandii – 10 m; 20 m when mature. Flattened branchlets bear tiny, scale-like leaves. Round cones are pea-sized. Needs room. Buy small (less than 1 m) plants. Cut hedges 3 times between late spring and early autumn.
C. l. 'Castlewellan' – 6 m. Yellow leaves.

C. leylandii

SITE & SOIL
4

PROPAGATION
1

FLOWER TIME
—

PRUNING
13 Spring

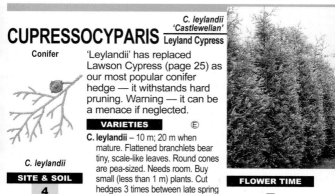

CUPRESSUS

C. macrocarpa 'Goldcrest'

Cypress

Conifer

Differs from the more popular Chamaecyparis by having branchlets which grow in all directions and cones which are large and leathery. Stake young trees and do not prune.

C. macrocarpa

| VARIETIES | Ⓔ |

C. sempervirens – 2.5 m. Column-like. Damaged by severe frosts.
C. arizonica – 2.5 m. Conical. Blue-grey leaves. Purple bark.
C. macrocarpa – 2.5 m. Cannot tolerate hard pruning.
C. m. 'Goldcrest' – 2.5 m; 7 m when mature. Yellow foliage. Conical. Most popular Cupressus.

SITE & SOIL
2

PROPAGATION
5

FLOWER TIME
—

PRUNING
14

CYTISUS

Broom

Shrub

During the flowering season the whippy stems and tiny leaves are covered with pea-like blooms. Nearly all are deciduous and both the bushy and tree-like forms need regular pruning. Cytisus will flourish in starved soil but there are several rules to follow. Always buy pot- or container-grown specimens and do not plant a variety or hybrid of C. scoparius in chalky soil. Always choose a sunny site. Despite all your care the plant is likely to become gaunt or die after about 10 years.

C. scoparius 'Andreanus'

C. kewensis

C. battandieri

C. praecox

C. purpureus

| VARIETIES | Ⓓ or Ⓢ Ⓔ |

C. scoparius – 1.5 m. Yellow. It is usual to choose a variety or hybrid. Examples include **C.s. 'Andreanus'** (Yellow/red) and **C. 'Burkwoodii'** (Yellow/red).
C. praecox – 1 m. Cream-yellow. Early flowering. Arching stems. Varieties include **C.p. 'Allgold'** (Yellow) and **C.p. 'Albus'** (White).
There are several ground-cover types which grow to 20 cm and need little pruning — look for **C. decumbens** (Yellow, late flowering).
Dwarf shrubs (45-60 cm) include **C. purpureus** (Lilac) and **C. kewensis** (Cream).
Tall species include **C. battandieri** (5 m. Yellow).

SITE & SOIL
1

PROPAGATION
1

FLOWER TIME
April — June

PRUNING
12   After flowering

DABOECIA

Shrub

D. cantabrica 'Alba'

D. cantabrica

SITE & SOIL
14

PROPAGATION
1

D. cantabrica 'Bicolor'
Irish Heath

It is surprising that Irish Heath is not more popular. The flower bells are larger than those of Erica and Calluna, and they appear from early summer to early autumn.

VARIETIES Ⓔ

D. cantabrica – 45 cm. Pale purple.
D. c. 'Alba' – White.
D. c. 'Atropurpurea' – Dark purple.
D. c. 'Bicolor' – White and purple on the same plant.
D. scotia 'Jack Drake' – 20 cm. Red.
D. s. 'William Buchanan' – 45 cm. Purple.

FLOWER TIME
June — October

PRUNING
10 After flowering

DANAE

Shrub

D. racemosa

SITE & SOIL
8

PROPAGATION
10

D. racemosa
Alexandrian Laurel

A plain-looking shrub with a useful feature — it will thrive and steadily spread in the dense shade under trees where little else will grow. The 'leaves' are flattened stems.

VARIETIES Ⓔ

D. racemosa (Ruscus racemosus) – 1 m. Greenish-yellow. 10 cm long 'leaves'. Small flowers appear in early summer, followed by orange berries in autumn. Arching stems. It will grow in both moist and dry situations. Closely related to the wildflower Butcher's Broom **(Ruscus aculeatus)**.

BERRY TIME
September — October

PRUNING
8 Spring

DAPHNE

Shrub

D. burkwoodii

SITE & SOIL
7

PROPAGATION
1

D. mezereum
Daphne

All the popular ones bear fragrant flowers followed by poisonous berries. February is the usual flowering time, but there are species which bloom in spring and summer.

VARIETIES Ⓓ or ⓈⒺ or Ⓔ

D. mezereum – 1 m. Purplish-red. February-March. Deciduous.
D. odora 'Marginata' – 1 m. Purplish-red. February-March. Cream-edged leaves. Evergreen.
D. burkwoodii – 1 m. Pink. May-June. Semi-evergreen.
D. tangutica – 60 cm. Pink-purple. May. Evergreen.

FLOWER TIME
Depends on species

PRUNING
2 After flowering

DAVIDIA

Tree

D. involucrata

D. involucrata
Handkerchief Tree

The common names (Handkerchief, Ghost and Dove Tree) all refer to the flower-heads — two large bracts surround the tiny blossoms.

VARIETIES Ⓓ

D. involucrata – 5 m; 15 m when mature. White. Leaves similar to lime, but are hairy below. Conical shape at first, later domed. Completely hardy despite exotic appearance. First flowers appear about 10 years after planting.

D. i. 'Vilmoriniana' – 5 m. White. Leaves are almost hairless.

SITE & SOIL	PROPAGATION
7	5

FLOWER TIME
May

PRUNING	
2	After flowering

DECAISNEA

Shrub

D. fargesii

D. fargesii
Blue Bean

An interesting rather than an attractive shrub with a unique feature. In autumn long blue pods hang from the branches. Stems may be damaged by late spring frosts.

VARIETIES Ⓓ

D. fargesii – 3 m. Yellowish-green. Bell-shaped flowers borne in 45 cm long clusters in May. 60 cm long leaves made up of bluish-green paired leaflets. Stout upright stems covered with a bluish bloom. Takes several years to reach pod-bearing stage. Pods are 12-30 cm long — size depends on summer weather.

SITE & SOIL	PROPAGATION
7	11

FRUITING TIME
September — October

PRUNING	
2	Spring

DESFONTAINIA

Shrub

D. spinosa

D. spinosa
Desfontainia

It may look like holly but it is much more difficult to grow. For Desfontainia to flourish it needs a reasonably mild site with a partially shaded wall nearby for protection.

VARIETIES Ⓔ

D. spinosa – 50 cm; 2 m when mature. Yellow-edged red. Flowers are 4 cm long trumpets. Spiny leaves are small and glossy. Buy a large specimen if possible as growth is very slow for the first 10 years. Mulch in May and keep the soil moist in summer.

D. s. 'Harold Comber' – All-red.

SITE & SOIL	PROPAGATION
6	1

FLOWER TIME
July — October

PRUNING	
2	Spring

36

DEUTZIA

Shrub

D. scabra

Deutzia

D. rosea

D. scabra 'Plena'

Give it room and the flowers will cover the whole bush. Easy to grow, but it needs watering during prolonged dry weather. Late frosts can damage flower buds.

VARIETIES ⒟

D. rosea – 1 m. Pink. May. Earliest to flower. Arching branches.
D. scabra – 2 m. White. June-July.
D. s. 'Plena' – 2 m. Rose/white. Double.
D. elegantissima 'Rosalind' – 1 m. Dark pink. May-June.
D. 'Magicien' – 2 m. White-edged pink. Large flowers. June.

SITE & SOIL	
3	

PROPAGATION	
3	

FLOWER TIME
Depends on species

PRUNING	
8	After flowering

DIPELTA

Shrub

D. floribunda

Dipelta

D. ventricosa

An uncommon shrub which looks like a large Weigela. Small clusters of trumpet-shaped blooms are borne above the long, pointed leaves. Difficult to propagate.

VARIETIES ⒟

D. floribunda – 2 m. Yellow-throated pale pink. Attractive peeling bark. Golden leaves in autumn. The most widely available species.
D. yunnanensis – 2 m. Orange-marked cream. Arching stems. Peeling bark.
D. ventricosa – 2 m. Orange-throated lilac-pink. Difficult to find.

SITE & SOIL	
3	

PROPAGATION	
3	

FLOWER TIME
May — June

PRUNING	
8	Late June

DORYCNIUM

Shrub

D. hirsutum

Canary Clover

D. hirsutum

Worth considering if you want a low-growing bush for a sunny sandy spot, especially if you like silvery plants. Do not feed — it blooms best under starvation conditions.

VARIETIES ⓈⒺ

D. hirsutum (Lotus hirsutum) – 60 cm. Pink-tinged white. Flower clusters appear on top of erect stems. Spread 1 m or more. Greyish-green leaves covered with silvery hairs. Reddish-brown seed pods. Stems are usually killed by frost in winter, so hard pruning is necessary every year.

SITE & SOIL	
20	

PROPAGATION	
1	

FLOWER TIME
June — September

PRUNING	
11	Early spring

ELAEAGNUS

Shrub

*E. ebbingei
'Gilt Edge'*
Elaeagnus

The flowers are fragrant but generally insignificant — Elaeagnus is grown for its foliage. Young leaves and shoots have a metallic sheen. Useful for hedging.

VARIETIES   Ⓓ or Ⓔ

*E. pungens
'Maculata'*

- **E. pungens 'Maculata'** – 2 m. White. Evergreen. Large leaves splashed with yellow.
- **E. ebbingei** – 3 m. Evergreen. Leathery grey-green leaves, silvery below. Orange berries. Useful for hedging.
- **E. e. 'Gilt Edge'** – Yellow-edged leaves.

SITE & SOIL
10

PROPAGATION
8

BERRY TIME
October — December

PRUNING
2   Spring

ELSHOLTZIA

Shrub

E. stauntonii
Mint Bush

A plant you will find in some catalogues but not at the garden centre — worth searching for if your soil is fertile and you want showy flower-heads in late summer.

VARIETIES   Ⓓ

E. stauntonii

- **E. stauntonii** – 1.2 m. Pink. Small flowers borne on 20 cm high slender spires. Dark green, toothed leaves emit a minty aroma when crushed. Yellow or red leaves in autumn. Stems usually killed by frost in winter, so hard pruning is necessary every year.
- **E. s. 'Alba'** – White. Rare.

SITE & SOIL
12

PROPAGATION
1

FLOWER TIME
August — October

PRUNING
11   Early spring

EMBOTHRIUM

Shrub

*E. coccineum
'Lanceolatum Norquinco'*
Chilean Fire Bush

The clusters of red spidery flowers on this tall plant are numerous enough to give it a 'burning bush' appearance — eye-catching but it is a fussy plant with special needs.

VARIETIES   Ⓔ

E. coccineum

- **E. coccineum** – 4.5 m. Orange-red. Narrow 4 cm long tubular blooms from which the styles protrude — tubes split and coil with age. Glossy leaves are oval. Needs humus-rich soil and wind protection. Suckers freely.
- **E. c. 'Lanceolatum Norquinco'** – Bright red.

SITE & SOIL
6

PROPAGATION
8

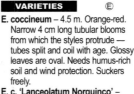
FLOWER TIME
May — June

PRUNING
1

ENKIANTHUS

Shrub

E. campanulatus
Pagoda Bush

If rhododendrons grow well in your garden then you will succeed with Enkianthus. This bush produces long-lasting flowers in spring and colourful leaves in autumn.

E. campanulatus

VARIETIES

E. campanulatus – 2 m. Red-edged yellow. Pendent bell-shaped flowers. Upper branches arranged in tiers. Yellow and red leaves in autumn.

E. cernus 'Rubens' – 1.5 m. Dark red. Reddish-purple leaves in autumn.

E. perulatus – 1.5 m. White.

ERICA

Shrub

Heath, Heather

It is easy to confuse the two popular heathers — Calluna and Erica. The leaves are tiny, the stems are wiry and the clustered blooms are urn-shaped. Erica, however, is more versatile in a number of ways. There is no standard flowering period — by careful selection you can have a bed in bloom all year round. Colours range from pure white to near black and there are lime-tolerant species as well as lime-hating ones. The basic rules are to plant firmly and to mulch around the plants with peat in late spring.

E. carnea

*E. carnea
'Springwood White'*

E. cinerea

VARIETIES

Lime-tolerant species:
E. carnea – 20 cm. Various. January-April. Varieties include **'Springwood White'** (White) and **'Vivellii'** (Dark red. Bronze leaves).
E. darleyensis – 60 cm. Various. November-April. Examples are **'Arthur Johnson'** (Pink) and **'Molten Silver'** (White).
Lime-hating species:
E. cinerea – 20-30 cm. Various. July-September. Examples are **'C.D. Easton'** (Pink) and **'Velvet Knight'** (Purple).
E. tetralix 'Pink Star' – 20 cm. Pink. June-October.
E. arborea – 1.2 m. White. March-May.

E. arborea

E. tetralix 'Pink Star'

ESCALLONIA

E. 'Donard Seedling'
Escallonia

Shrub

Upright at first and then arching downwards, the stems are clothed with small, shiny leaves. Small, bell-shaped flowers cover the bush in summer.

VARIETIES ⓈⒺ or Ⓔ

E. 'Apple Blossom'

E. **'Apple Blossom'** – 1.5 m. White/pink. Slow growing.

E. **'Donard Seedling'** – 2.5 m. White. Pink buds. Hardier than E. 'Apple Blossom'.

E. **'Iveyi'** – 3 m. White. August. Needs wall protection.

E. rubra **'Macrantha'** – 3 m. Red. Vigorous. Useful for hedging.

SITE & SOIL
10

PROPAGATION
1

FLOWER TIME
June — September

PRUNING
8   Autumn

EUCALYPTUS

E. gunnii
Gum Tree

Tree
•
Shrub

E. gunnii is the only popular species. You can prune it each year to maintain the blue juvenile foliage or you can let it grow as a tree with grey-green adult foliage.

VARIETIES   Ⓔ

E. **gunnii** – 15 m when mature. Cider Gum. Oval juvenile leaves replaced by sickle-shaped ones as the plant matures.

E. **pauciflora 'Niphophila'** – 7 m. Snow Gum. Glossy grey-green leaves. Attractive bark.

E. **dalrympleana** – 15 m. Bronze juvenile leaves.

E. gunnii

SITE & SOIL
9

PROPAGATION
5

FLOWER TIME
—

PRUNING
2   Spring

EUCRYPHIA

E. nymansensis 'Nymansay'
Eucryphia

Shrub

Showy but not often seen. There are two problems — it becomes tree-like in time and so needs space, and it is not easy to grow. Plant it close to a wall.

VARIETIES   Ⓓ or Ⓔ

E. **nymansensis 'Nymansay'** – 3 m; 8 m when mature. White. Masses of 8 cm wide flowers in late summer. Evergreen.

E. **milliganii** – 2.5 m. White. Evergreen.

E. **glutinosa** – 3 m. White. Abundant flowers. Deciduous. Good autumn colour.

E. glutinosa

SITE & SOIL
6

PROPAGATION
2

FLOWER TIME
July — September

PRUNING
2   April

EUONYMUS

E. europaeus
Spindleberry

Shrub

Tall shrubs with colourful autumn foliage and fruits. The greenish flowers in spring are insignificant. Grow several if possible to ensure cross-pollination.

E. alatus

SITE & SOIL
10

PROPAGATION
1

VARIETIES   ⒟

E. europaeus – 4 m. Common Spindle. 2 cm wide lobed red fruits split open to reveal orange seeds. Pink or red leaves in autumn.
E. e. 'Red Cascade' – 3 m. Brighter fruits than the species.
E. alatus – 1.5 m. Bright red leaves in autumn. Winged stems.
E. a. 'Compactus' – 80 cm. Dwarf.

FRUITING TIME
October — December

PRUNING
2   Late spring

EUONYMUS

E. fortunei
'Emerald 'n' Gold'
Euonymus

Shrub

The evergreen group are more popular than the deciduous species. A must for any shrub border — there are variegated ground-covering varieties and bushy forms for hedging.

E. japonicus
'Aureopictus'

SITE & SOIL
10

PROPAGATION
1/3

VARIETIES   ⒠

E. fortunei – 1 m. Good ground cover.
E. f. 'Emerald 'n' Gold' – Gold-edged leaves.
E. f. 'Blondy' – Yellow-hearted leaves.
E. japonicus – 2 m.
E. j. 'Aureopictus' – Yellow-hearted leaves.

FLOWER TIME
—

PRUNING
2   Spring

EXOCHORDA

E. macrantha
'The Bride'
Pearl Bush

Shrub

An attractive bush when in bloom with flowers on short spikes festooning the arching branches. There is a draw-back — the flowering period lasts for only 7-10 days.

E. racemosa

SITE & SOIL
2

PROPAGATION
2/8

VARIETIES   ⒟

E. giraldii 'Wilsonii' – 3 m. White. Large flowers. Arching branches.
E. racemosa – 4 m when mature. White. Smaller flowers than E. giraldii 'Wilsonii'. Spreading growth habit.
E. macrantha 'The Bride' – 2 m. White. Abundant flowers. Compact rounded growth habit.

FLOWER TIME
May

PRUNING
10   After flowering

FABIANA

Shrub

F. imbricata 'Violacea'

F. imbricata

F. imbricata 'Violacea'

Fabiana

An unusual shrub which looks like a Tree Heath (Erica arborea), but they are not related. Wiry stems bear tiny leaves and a profusion of small flowers in early summer.

VARIETIES   Ⓔ

F. imbricata – 2 m. White. Plume-like flower-heads. Blooms are long open-mouthed tubes. Upright growth habit.

F. i. 'Violacea' – 2 m. Lavender. Growth more spreading than the species.

F. i. 'Prostrata' – 1 m. Mauve-tinged white. Hardier than the species.

SITE & SOIL
20

PROPAGATION
2

FLOWER TIME
May — June

PRUNING
2   July

FAGUS

Tree

F. sylvatica 'Purpurea Pendula'

SITE & SOIL
10

PROPAGATION
5/12

F. sylvatica

Beech

There are stately specimens in parks, and beech hedges in countless gardens — in addition there are colourful varieties for lawns and large plots. Little will grow below.

VARIETIES   Ⓓ

F. sylvatica – 8 m; 30 m when mature. Common Beech. Wavy-edged leaves. Use as a hedge.

F. s. 'Dawyck' – 6 m. Column-shaped.

F. s. 'Pendula' – 5 m. Weeping habit.

F. s. 'Purpurea Pendula' – 5 m. Weeping Copper Beech.

F. s. 'Zlatia' – 5 m. Golden Beech.

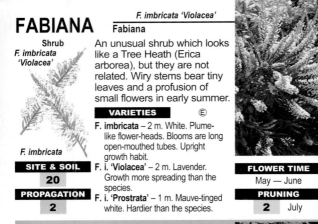

FLOWER TIME
—

PRUNING
2   Summer

FATSIA

Shrub

F. japonica

SITE & SOIL
15

PROPAGATION
1

F. japonica 'Variegata'

Castor Oil Plant

A plant with large decorative leaves for a sunless spot. Flower-heads appear in autumn. Buy it from the shrub section and not the house plant department.

VARIETIES   Ⓔ

F. japonica – 3 m. Cream. Tiny blooms in globular heads are followed by black berries. 30 cm wide deeply-lobed shiny leaves on long stalks. Quite hardy despite its exotic appearance.

F. j. 'Variegata' – 3 m. Cream. White-edged leaves. Less hardy than the species.

FLOWER TIME
October — November

PRUNING
2   Spring

FORSYTHIA

Golden Bells

Shrub

F. intermedia
'Spectabilis'

Gardens are brightened in spring by the masses of yellow flowers on the leafless branches. The blooms are widely-flared shallow bells in colours ranging from palest yellow to amber. There are varieties to clothe walls, to cover bare ground, to provide hedges and to stand alone as specimen bushes. Fully hardy and easy to grow, but there are two enemies — birds which strip off flower buds and people who shorten all the branches in summer to 'keep it tidy' which results in lots of growth and few flowers next year.

F. intermedia 'Spectabilis'

F. intermedia
'Lynwood'

VARIETIES ⒹⓄ

F. intermedia – 3 m. Yellow. Very popular. Upright growth habit. A variety is the usual choice: **'Spectabilis'** — Narrow, twisted petals. **'Lynwood'** — Broader petals, freer flowering.

F. suspensa – 4 m. Yellow. Weak stems — provide support. The variety **'Nymans'** has red stems.

F. 'Beatrix Farrand' – 3.5 m. Orange-yellow. Large blooms. Purplish-red leaves in autumn.

F. suspensa

F. 'Beatrix Farrand'

SITE & SOIL
10

PROPAGATION
3

F. ovata 'Tetragold' – 2 m. Amber.

F. 'Fiesta' – 1 m. Golden yellow. Yellow-centred leaves. Compact. There are several other dwarfs. Look for **F. 'Golden Nugget'** and **F. viridissima 'Bronxensis'**.

FLOWER TIME
March — April

PRUNING	
8	After flowering

FOTHERGILLA

F. major
'Monticola'

Fothergilla

Shrub

Bottle brush flower-heads appear before the leaves in spring to provide an unusual display. It comes into its own in autumn with bright yellow, orange or red foliage.

VARIETIES Ⓓ

F. gardenii – 1 m. White. Small fragrant flower-heads. Growth not robust.

F. major

F. major – 2 m. White. Flower-heads larger than F. gardenii. Yellow, gold and orange leaves in autumn.

SITE & SOIL
14

PROPAGATION
6

F. m. 'Monticola' – 2 m. White. Very similar to the species but autumn leaves are predominantly red.

FLOWER TIME
April — May

PRUNING	
2	Winter

43

FRAXINUS

Tree

F. excelsior 'Pendula'

Ash

The Common Ash is not suitable for the average garden — it is late coming into leaf and it is too tall. There are more compact types which will thrive almost anywhere.

F. excelsior

VARIETIES ⒟

F. excelsior – 10 m; 20 m when mature. Common Ash. Bunches of fruits (keys) in summer.

F. e. 'Jaspidea' – 5 m. Golden Ash. Leaves yellow in spring and autumn. Yellow bark.

F. e. 'Pendula' – 5 m. Weeping Ash.

F. ornus – 5 m. White flowers in May. Purple leaves in autumn.

SITE & SOIL
10

PROPAGATION
5/12

FLOWER TIME
—

PRUNING
2   Late winter

FREMONTODENDRON

Shrub

F. californicum

Flannel Flower

A showy wall shrub with large flowers all summer long and lobed leathery leaves all year round. Warning — the down on leaves and stems can irritate the skin.

F. californicum

VARIETIES ⓈⒺ or Ⓔ

F. californicum – 4 m. Yellow. 6 cm wide saucer-shaped flowers. 10 cm long 3-lobed leaves.

F. 'California Glory' – 4 m. Yellow. Flowers flushed red on the outside. Semi-evergreen. Plant against a south-facing wall.

F. 'Pacific Sunset' – 5 m. Dark orange fading to yellow.

SITE & SOIL
2

PROPAGATION
2

FLOWER TIME
May — September

PRUNING
2   Spring

FUCHSIA

Shrub

F. magellanica 'Alba'

Species Fuchsia

F. magellanica and its varieties can be grown outdoors to produce arching branches and pendent bell-like flowers year after year. Mulch over crowns in winter.

F. magellanica 'Riccartonii'

VARIETIES ⒟

F. magellanica – 2 m. Red/purple. Usual to choose a variety. Flowers are narrower than the hybrid varieties — see page 45.

F. m. 'Riccartonii' – Red/purple. Hardiest variety. Old favourite.

F. m. 'Alba' – Mauve-tinged white.

F. m. 'Gracilis Aurea' – Red. Yellow leaves.

SITE & SOIL
7

PROPAGATION
4

FLOWER TIME
July — October

PRUNING
18   April

44

FUCHSIA

Shrub

F. 'Mrs. Popple'

F. 'Alice Hoffman'

Hybrid Fuchsia

Apart from F. magellanica and its varieties (see page 44) there are numerous hybrids which are hardy enough to be grown outdoors. Mulch the crowns in winter.

VARIETIES Ⓓ

F. **'Alice Hoffman'** – 60 cm. Red/white.
F. **'Doctor Foster'** – 90 cm. Red/violet. Very large flowers.
F. **'Madame Cornelissen'** – 80 cm. Red/white.
F. **'Margaret'** – 1.5 m. Red/purple.
F. **'Mrs. Popple'** – 80 cm. Red/violet.
F. **'Tom Thumb'** – 40 cm. Violet/red.

FLOWER TIME
July — October
PRUNING
18   April

GARRYA

Shrub

G. elliptica

G. elliptica 'James Roof'

Silk Tassel Bush

Grow this tall shrub against a wall or trellis for its winter interest — long and slender tassels hang from the branches. Flourishes in poor soil, coastal areas and shade.

VARIETIES Ⓔ

G. **elliptica** – 3.5 m. Cream. 20 cm long tassel-like catkins which are grey-green at first.
G. e. **'James Roof'** – 3.5 m. Cream. Tassels thicker than the species and up to 35 cm long.
G. **issaquahensis 'Pat Ballard'** – 3.5 m. 20 cm long tassels are purplish-green.

FLOWER TIME
January — February
PRUNING
2   Spring

GAULTHERIA

Shrub

G. shallon

G. procumbens

Wintergreen

A carpeter for planting under lime-hating plants such as rhododendrons and camellias — there are year-round glossy leaves, summer flowers and autumn berries.

VARIETIES Ⓔ

G. **procumbens** – 20 cm. White. Checkerberry. Lily of the Valley-like flowers. Red berries in September-October. Oval leaves.
G. **cuneata** – 50 cm. White. White berries. Narrow leaves.
G. **shallon** – 1.5 m. Pink-edged white. Dark purple berries. Forms a dense thicket.

FLOWER TIME
June — July
PRUNING
2   Early spring

GENISTA

Shrub

Broom

This group of brooms generally have wiry stems, tiny leaves and pea-like flowers in summer. All bloom freely if given plenty of sun and no fertilizer.

VARIETIES ⓓ

G. lydia – 60 cm. Yellow. May-June. Arching stems.

G. hispanica – 30 cm. Yellow. June-July. Spiny branches.

G. pilosa 'Vancouver Gold' – 25 cm. Yellow. May. Prostrate growth habit. Thornless.

G. aetnensis – 4 m. Yellow. July-August.

G. lydia

SITE & SOIL
20

PROPAGATION
7

FLOWER TIME
Depends on species

PRUNING
13   After flowering

GINKGO

G. biloba

Conifer

Maidenhair Tree

Ginkgo is a conifer, despite its broad leaves, plum-like fruits and leaves which fall in winter. Conical at first, it later becomes a graceful, spreading tree.

VARIETIES ⓓ

G. biloba – 3 m; 18 m when mature. Fan-shaped 2-lobed leaves, pale green turning yellow in autumn. Small yellow fruit may occasionally appear. Slow-growing at first — later quick-growing. Varieties are hard to find.

G. b. 'Fastigiata' – Column-like.

G. b. 'Pendula' – Weeping branches.

G. biloba

SITE & SOIL
10

PROPAGATION
5

FLOWER TIME
—

PRUNING
1

GLEDITSIA

G. triacanthos 'Sunburst'

Tree

Honey Locust

A graceful tree grown for its attractive leaves, which appear late in the season, and its long seed pods. Most types have trunks with thorns. Good drought and shade tolerance.

VARIETIES ⓓ

G. triacanthos – 8 m. Yellow leaves in autumn. Strong thorns on trunk. Quick-growing.

G. t. 'Ruby Lace' – 5 m. Young leaves red, maturing to bronzy-green. Ferny foliage.

G. t. 'Sunburst' – 5 m. Young leaves yellow, maturing to greenish-yellow. Thornless.

G. triacanthos 'Sunburst'

SITE & SOIL
10

PROPAGATION
7

FLOWER TIME
—

PRUNING
2   Spring

GREVILLEA

G. alpina
'Olympic Flame'

Spider Flower

Shrub

Usually regarded as a conservatory plant which is stood outdoors in summer, but there are a few which can be grown against a south-facing wall in a mild area.

VARIETIES Ⓢ or Ⓔ

G. juniperina 'Sulphurea'
'Sulphurea'

VARIETIES Ⓢ or Ⓔ

G. juniperina 'Sulphurea' – 2 m. Yellow. May-June. Flower-heads are made up of tubular blooms with curled-back lobes and prominent styles.

G. rosmarinifolia – 2 m. Cream-edged red. June-August.

G. alpina 'Olympic Flame' – 1.2 m. Cream/red. April-May.

SITE & SOIL
9

PROPAGATION
1

FLOWER TIME
Depends on species

PRUNING	
2	After flowering

GRISELINIA

G. littoralis 'Variegata'

Griselinia

Shrub

A vigorous upright shrub with leathery evergreen leaves for a number of difficult situations — it will thrive in chalky soil, dense shade and salt-laden air. Can be used for hedging.

VARIETIES Ⓔ

G. littoralis
'Dixon's Cream'

G. littoralis – 3 m. Oval leaves. Some leaves may be damaged by frost.

G. l. 'Dixon's Cream' – 3 m. Cream-hearted green leaves. Needs more light than the species.

G. l. 'Variegata' – 3 m. Cream-edged green leaves. Needs more light than the species.

SITE & SOIL
10

PROPAGATION
1

FLOWER TIME
—

PRUNING	
2	Spring

HALESIA

H. carolina

Silverbell

Shrub
•
Tree

The clusters of snowdrop-like flowers which appear before the leaves open are followed by winged green fruits. Easy to grow in acid soil, but it is not often seen.

VARIETIES Ⓓ

H. monticola

H. carolina (H. tetraptera) – 2.5 m. White. Snowdrop Tree. Small pear-shaped fruits. Leaves yellow in autumn. Tree-like when mature.

H. monticola – 3 m. White. Mountain Silverbell. 3 cm wide flowers. 5 cm long fruits.

H. m. 'Vestita' – 3 m. Pink-tinged white.

SITE & SOIL
17

PROPAGATION
1

FLOWER TIME
May

PRUNING	
2	After flowering

H. intermedia 'Jelena'

HAMAMELIS

Witch Hazel

Shrub

Spidery flowers appear on leafless stems for many weeks in winter, after which there are hazel-like leaves. Autumn foliage takes on attractive tints.

VARIETIES   ⒟

H. mollis – 2.5 m. Yellow. Chinese Witch Hazel. Large fragrant flowers. Yellow leaves in autumn.
H. m. 'Pallida' – Yellow.
H. m. 'Brevipetala' – Bronzy-yellow.
H. intermedia 'Jelena' – 2.5 m. Orange. Red leaves in autumn.
H. i. 'Diane' – Red. Orange or red leaves in autumn.

H. mollis 'Pallida'

SITE & SOIL
9

PROPAGATION
5

FLOWER TIME
December — February

PRUNING
2   After flowering

HEBE

Shrubby Veronica

Shrub

These popular evergreens can be divided into 3 groups. The Whipcord Hebes have scale-like leaves and the remainder have oval ones. These leafy varieties are either Low-growing Hebes which reach no more than 45 cm or Tall-growing Hebes which exceed 45 cm. A typical leafy Hebe is a compact bush with dense foliage and spikes of white or blue flowers. Some but not all are hardy — the larger the leaf, the more tender the variety is likely to be. Tenderness apart, Hebes are easy plants to grow.

H. 'Carl Teschner'

VARIETIES   ⒠

Whipcord Hebes:
  H. armstrongii – 80 cm. White. May-June. Yellowish-green leaves.
Low-growing Hebes:
  H. pinguifolia 'Pagei' – 30 cm. White. May-August.
  H. 'Red Edge' – 45 cm. White. June-July. Red-edged grey-green leaves.
  H. 'Carl Teschner' – 25 cm. Violet. June-July.
Tall-growing Hebes:
  H. 'Autumn Glory' – 80 cm. Violet. June-October. Green leaves.
  H. 'Great Orme' – 80 cm. Pink. July-October. Green leaves.
  H. 'Mrs. Winder' – 60 cm. Blue. June-September. Purple leaves.

H. armstrongii

H. pinguifolia 'Pagei'

H. 'Great Orme'

H. 'Autumn Glory'

SITE & SOIL
2

PROPAGATION
1

FLOWER TIME
Depends on variety

PRUNING
19   May

HEDERA

Climber

H. helix 'Goldheart'

H. hibernica

H. colchica

Ivy

Usually regarded as a house plant or a tree-damaging weed, but if you choose wisely and prune properly it is a reliable and colourful climber. Ivy is evergreen and will grow anywhere — a rare combination among climbers. Neither trees nor sound brickwork is damaged, but you must keep it in check. Brightly-coloured variegated types are available, and these provide useful ground cover between deciduous shrubs. The leaves are often deeply cut but they become smooth-edged and oval as the plant ages.

VARIETIES (E)

H. helix – Triangular, 3- or 5-lobed leaves. Dark green and glossy. Common Ivy. Choose a variety: **'Green Ripple'** (Deeply-cut, green), **'Buttercup'** (All-yellow), **'Glacier'** (White-edged grey-green), **'Goldheart'** (Yellow-centred green).
H. hibernica – Vigorous. 5-lobed leaves. Irish Ivy. Useful for covering walls.
H. colchica – Large leaves. Dark green. Useful for ground cover. **'Dentata Variegata'** (Yellow-edged green), **'Sulphur Heart'** (Yellow-centred green).
H. canariensis 'Variegata' – Large leaves. Cream-splashed green. Red stems. Not completely hardy.

H. helix 'Buttercup'

H. helix 'Glacier'

FLOWER TIME
—

PRUNING
13 Spring & summer

HEDYSARUM

H. coronarium
Hedysarum

Shrub

H. coronarium

It is surprising that this shrub is not more widely grown. All it needs is a sunny site and soil which is not heavy to produce a showy summer-long floral display.

VARIETIES (D)

H. coronarium – 1.2 m. Red. French Honeysuckle. Pea-like blooms are borne on spikes — flower-heads can be used for indoor decoration.
H. multijugum – 2 m. Rosy-purple. Mongolian Sweet Vetch. Flower spikes are up to 30 cm long. Leaves are made up of oval leaflets. Not easy to find.

FLOWER TIME
July — September

PRUNING
8 Early spring

HELIANTHEMUM

H. 'Wisley Pink'
Sun Rose

Shrub

The papery blooms of this low-growing shrub form a sheet of colour for many weeks in summer, but each bloom lasts for only a day or two. Annual pruning is important.

VARIETIES Ⓔ

There are many named hybrids:
The Wisley Series (20 cm. **H. 'Wisley White'**, **'Wisley Pink'** etc) have silvery-grey leaves.
The Ben Series (20 cm. **H. 'Ben Hope'** etc) are neat and hardy.
H. 'Fire Dragon' – 20 cm. Orange.
H. 'Raspberry Ripple' – 20 cm. White-edged pink.

H. 'Fire Dragon'

SITE & SOIL
20

PROPAGATION
1

FLOWER TIME
May — July

PRUNING
10 After flowering

HELICHRYSUM

H. italicum 'Serotinum'
Shrubby Helichrysum

Shrub

The leaves are woolly or densely hairy and sometimes aromatic. The flowers are button-like and are borne in clusters — they can be cut and dried.

VARIETIES Ⓔ

H. italicum – 60 cm. Yellow. Grey-green leaves. Woolly stems.
H. i. 'Serotinum' – 45 cm. Yellow. Grey needle-like leaves emit curry-like smell when crushed.
H. splendidum – 90 cm. Yellow. Grey leaves. 'Everlasting' flowers dry on the plant.
H. milfordiae – 8 cm. White.

H. splendidum

SITE & SOIL
20

PROPAGATION
1

FLOWER TIME
June — August

PRUNING
11 Spring

HIBISCUS

H. syriacus 'Red Heart'
Shrubby Mallow

Shrub

In late summer the upright branches are clothed with large, saucer-shaped blooms. It needs sunshine, good drainage and protection from cold winds.

VARIETIES Ⓓ

H. syriacus – 2.5 m. Various.
H. s. 'Blue Bird' – Dark-eyed violet.
H. s. 'Woodbridge' – Dark-eyed pink.
H. s. 'Red Heart' – Red-eyed white.
H. s. 'Hamabo' – Red-eyed white.
H. s. 'Lady Stanley' – Red-eyed white. Double — may disappoint in wet weather.

H. syriacus 'Blue Bird'

SITE & SOIL
1

PROPAGATION
5

FLOWER TIME
July — September

PRUNING
2 Early spring

HIPPOPHAE

Sea Buckthorn

Shrub

H. rhamnoides

SITE & SOIL
3

PROPAGATION
6/8

Sea Buckthorn has a number of virtues. It will flourish in any well-drained soil and is unaffected by salt-laden air, strong winds, starved soil or periods of drought.

VARIETIES ⓓ

H. rhamnoides – 4 m if left unpruned, but can be pruned regularly for hedging. Silvery willow-like leaves. Insignificant flowers in March-April — orange berries untouched by birds. Bushes are single-sexed — plant male and female specimens close together for berry production.

BERRY TIME
September — February

PRUNING
2 Summer

HYDRANGEA

Hydrangea

Shrub
•
Climber

H. macrophylla:
Mophead

H. macrophylla:
Lacecap

H. petiolaris

H. paniculata
'Grandiflora'

SITE & SOIL
22

PROPAGATION
1

The large flower-heads are borne in late summer when the border is often short of colour. Most popular are the Mopheads with ball-like blooms — less common are the Lacecaps with a flat flower-head made up of an outer ring of large flowers and a central group of much smaller blooms. There are other types, including bushes with cone-shaped flower-heads and climbers with lacecap-type flowers. Hydrangeas need good soil, water during dry spells and regular feeding.

H. macrophylla 'Hamburg'

VARIETIES ⓓ

H. macrophylla is the usual parent. Average height 1.5 m. Acid conditions needed for blue flowers.
Mopheads include **'Hamburg'** (Pink or blue, depending on soil pH), **'Ayesha'** (Pink or mauve) and **'Madame Emile Moulliere'** (White).
Lacecaps include **'Blue Wave'** (Pink or blue), **'Mariesii'** (Pink or blue) and **'Geoffrey Chadbund'** (Red).
H. paniculata 'Grandiflora' – 2.5 m. White. Cone-shaped flower-heads.
H. arborescens 'Annabelle' – 1.2 m. White.
H. 'Preziosa' – 1.2 m. Pink changing to red.
H. petiolaris – Can reach 20 m x 20 m. White. Self-clinging climber.

H. macrophylla 'Blue Wave'

FLOWER TIME
July — September

PRUNING
20

HYPERICUM

St. John's Wort

Shrub

H. calycinum

H. inodorum 'Elstead'

H. 'Hidcote'

H. polyphyllum

The one you are most likely to see is Rose of Sharon — a low-growing shrub which spreads rapidly in sun or shade. Most or all the leaves are retained in winter and the floral display lasts from mid-summer to the first frosts — the blooms are flat discs with a central boss of stamens. Other species are available, with heights ranging from 10 cm to 2 m. All the flowers are quite similar and some produce attractive berries. Some are much less invasive than Rose of Sharon, but a few are rather tender.

H. calycinum

VARIETIES ⓈⒺ or Ⓔ

H. calycinum – 45 cm. Yellow. Rose of Sharon. Will grow in any soil which does not waterlog.

H. moserianum 'Tricolor' – 60 cm. Yellow. Small flowers. Less invasive. Green/cream/pink leaves.

H. inodorum 'Elstead' – 1 m. Yellow. Small flowers. Elongated red berries.

H. androsaemum – 1 m. Yellow. Black berries. Red autumn leaves.

H. 'Hidcote' – 1.5 m. Yellow. 8 cm wide flowers. Large leaves.

H. 'Rowallane' – 2 m. Yellow. Impressive but rather tender.

H. polyphyllum – 15 cm. Yellow.

H. p. 'Citrinum' – 10 cm. Lemon yellow.

H. moserianum 'Tricolor'

SITE & SOIL		FLOWER TIME
10		June — October

PROPAGATION		PRUNING
1		**21**

ILEX

I. aquifolium 'Golden Queen'

Holly

Shrub
•
Tree

I. aquifolium 'Argentea Marginata'

There are varieties which differ from the Christmas card picture — you can find smooth-edged and yellow-splashed leaves and both gold and black berries.

VARIETIES Ⓔ

I. aquifolium – 3 m. **'Golden Queen'** (Male. Yellow-edged green), **'Argenta Marginata'** (Female. Silver-edged green) and **'J.C. van Tol'** (Female/male).

I. altaclerensis 'Golden King' – 2 m. Female. Yellow-edged green.

I. crenata 'Golden Gem' – Small box-like leaves — yellow in spring.

SITE & SOIL		BERRY TIME
10		October — December

PROPAGATION		PRUNING	
6		**13**	Spring or summer

INDIGOFERA

I. heterantha

Indigo

Shrub

I. heterantha

I. heterantha

Graceful spikes of pale purple flowers appear from July until October, but the stems are bare until late May. Stems may be killed by winter frost but regrowth occurs.

VARIETIES   Ⓓ

I. heterantha – 1.5 m; more if grown against a south-facing wall. Rosy-purple. Flower-heads of pea-like blooms arise in the leaf axils. Leaves are made up of oval leaflets. Open bush with long, arching stems.

I. amblyantha – 1.5 m. Pink. 15 cm long flower spikes. Hard to find.

SITE & SOIL
1

PROPAGATION
1

FLOWER TIME
July — October

PRUNING
12   April

ITEA

I. illicifolia

Sweetspire

Shrub

I. illicifolia

Both species produce small, fragrant white flowers, both are slow to establish and neither is a popular shrub. The similarities end there — they are quite different.

VARIETIES   Ⓓ or Ⓔ

I. illicifolia – 2.5 m. White. August-September. Holly-leaf Sweetspire. Evergreen. 30 cm long catkin-like tassels. Holly-like leaves.

I. virginica – 1.2 m. White. July. Virginia Sweetspire. Deciduous. Upright cylindrical flower-heads. Oval smooth-edged leaves turn red in autumn.

SITE & SOIL
10

PROPAGATION
1

FLOWER TIME
Depends on species

PRUNING
2   April

JASMINUM

J. nudiflorum

Jasmine

Shrub
•
Climber

J. officinale 'Grandiflorum'

There are 2 groups. The Bushy Jasmines generally have weak stems and may need support — the Climbing Jasmines have twining stems.

VARIETIES   Ⓓ or ⓈⒺ or Ⓔ

Bushy Jasmines:
J. nudiflorum – 3 m. Yellow. November-February. Winter Jasmine. Needs support. Popular.
J. humile 'Revolutum' – 2 m. Yellow. May-July. Evergreen.
Climbing Jasmines:
J. officinale 'Grandiflorum' – 8 m. White. July-September.

SITE & SOIL
11

PROPAGATION
1

FLOWER TIME
Depends on species

PRUNING
22

J. regia

JUGLANS

Tree

Walnut

J. regia

A walnut tree is grown for its shape and shade effect and/or for its edible fruit. Unfortunately walnuts do not appear for about 15 years and a good spring is required.

VARIETIES (D)

J. regia – 8 m; 20 m when mature. Common Walnut. Large divided leaves appear in late spring.

J. r. 'Lacianata' – 6 m; 15 m when mature. Deeply-cut leaves. Drooping branches.

J. nigra – 8 m; 25 m when mature. Black Walnut. Dark green divided leaves. Black stems and fruit.

SITE & SOIL
1

PROPAGATION
5

FRUITING TIME
October

PRUNING
2 Summer or autumn

JUNIPERUS

Conifer

Juniper

J. virginiana 'Skyrocket'

The wide range of shapes and their ease of cultivation make these conifers deservedly popular. There are ground-hugging types in green, grey, blue and yellow as well as medium-sized shrubs and tall-growing trees. All are hardy and tolerant of poor conditions. Alkaline, acid and stony soils do not pose a problem, and they withstand drought better than most conifers. Scale-like adult leaves and needle-like juvenile ones may occur on the same branch. The cones are pea-sized with fleshy scales.

J. communis 'Depressa Aur

VARIETIES (E)

J. squamata 'Blue Star' – 40 cm. Silvery-blue.
J. s. 'Meyeri' – 1.2 m. Drooping branch tips. Blue.
J. media 'Pfitzerana' – 1.2 m. Strong branches rising at 45° — tips droop gracefully. Shade-resistant.
J. m. 'Old Gold' – 1 m. Spread to 2.5 m. Bronzy-gold.
J. communis 'Compressa' – 30 cm. Column-like.
J. c. 'Hibernica' – 3 m. Irish Juniper. Narrow column-like.
J. c. 'Depressa Aurea' – 30 cm. Gold. Bronze in winter.
J. horizontalis 'Glauca' – 30 cm. Wide-spreading, reaching 3 m or more. Whipcord-like tips. Steely blue.
J. virginiana 'Skyrocket' – 2 m; 5 m when mature. Narrow column-like. Blue-grey.

J. chinensis 'Pyramidalis' – 2 m. Conical. Blue-green.
J. sabina 'Tamariscifolia' – 30 cm. Horizontal branches.
J. procumbens 'Nana' – 20 cm. Branch ends turn upwards.

SITE & SOIL
10

PROPAGATION
5/3

J. chinensis 'Pyramidalis

FLOWER TIME
—

PRUNING
2 Midsummer

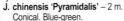

KALMIA

Shrub

K. latifolia

K. latifolia

Kalmia

Easily mistaken for a rhododendron when not in flower, but the blooms are quite different. The buds look like chinese lanterns and the flowers have crimped edges.

VARIETIES Ⓔ

K. latifolia – 2.5 m. Pink. Calico Bush. 15 cm wide flower-heads. Hardy but fussy — needs moist peaty soil, protection from cold winds and a late spring mulch. Takes several years before flowering freely.

K. angustifolia 'Rubra' – 1 m. Rose-red. Azalea-like when not in bloom.

FLOWER TIME
May — June

PRUNING
1

SITE & SOIL
14

PROPAGATION
1

KERRIA

Shrub

K. japonica

*K. japonica
'Pleniflora'*

K. japonica 'Pleniflora'

Jew's Mallow

Produces masses of flowers in spring and occasionally blooms in summer and autumn. It will grow almost anywhere but needs annual pruning.

VARIETIES Ⓓ

K. japonica – 2 m. Yellow. Single. 5 cm wide flowers. Arching stems. Good free-standing shrub.

K. j. 'Golden Guinea' – Extra large flowers.

K. j. 'Pleniflora' – 2.5 m. Yellow. Double. Good wall shrub.

K. j. 'Variegata' – 1 m. Yellow. Single. Cream-edged green leaves.

FLOWER TIME
April — May

PRUNING
10   June

SITE & SOIL
16

PROPAGATION
3/8

KOELREUTERIA

Tree

K. paniculata

K. paniculata

Pride of India

Trees which bear bright flowers in midsummer are unusual, yet this example has never become popular. One problem is that it needs a good summer to flower freely.

VARIETIES Ⓓ

K. paniculata – 5 m. Yellow. Golden Rain Tree. 30 cm long upright spikes of 4-petalled flowers. Colourful leaves made up of toothed leaflets appear late — pink at first, bluish-green later and yellow in autumn. Bladder-like fruits are pink when mature. Varieties such as the upright **'Fastigiata'** are rare.

FLOWER TIME
July — August

PRUNING
2   Spring

SITE & SOIL
1

PROPAGATION
5

KOLKWITZIA

K. amabilis
'Pink Cloud'

Beauty Bush

Shrub

Bell-shaped flowers festoon the arching stems of this easy-to-grow and hardy shrub. It looks rather like a tall Weigela but it has none of its rival's popularity.

K. amabilis

VARIETIES   Ⓓ

K. amabilis – 3 m if left unpruned. Yellow-throated pink. Grey-green leaves. Regular pruning is necessary — keep at 1.5-2 m. Quick-growing — can be used for hedging. Peeling brown bark provides winter interest.

K. a. 'Pink Cloud' – Darker pink and more popular than the species.

SITE & SOIL
11

PROPAGATION
1

FLOWER TIME
May — June

PRUNING
10   After flowering

LABURNUM

L. watereri 'Vossii'

Golden Rain

Tree

A light and graceful tree casting dappled shade. The long flower sprays are followed by brown pods below the shiny green branches. Leaves, twigs and seeds are poisonous.

L. anagyroides

VARIETIES   Ⓓ

L. anagyroides – 5 m. Yellow. Common Laburnum.

L. watereri 'Vossii' – 5 m. Yellow. Sprays up to 50 cm long — flowers larger and darker than above. The most popular Laburnum.

L. alpinum 'Pendulum' – 3 m. Yellow. Slow-growing. Weeping branches reach the ground.

SITE & SOIL
10

PROPAGATION
5

FLOWER TIME
May — June

PRUNING
2   After flowering

LAPAGERIA

L. rosea

Chilean Bellflower

Climber

Try it outdoors if you like a challenge — it will survive against a wall if your garden is relatively frost-free. The large flowers make the risk worthwhile.

L. rosea

VARIETIES   Ⓔ

L. rosea – 3 m. Rose-red. 8 cm long waxy-petalled pendent flowers borne singly or in clusters of 2 or 3. Leathery oblong leaves. Twining stems. Shade from midday sun is essential. Mulch in winter.

L. r. 'Nash Court' – Red-blotched pink.

L. r. 'Albiflora' – White.

SITE & SOIL
6

PROPAGATION
6

FLOWER TIME
July — October

PRUNING
2   Spring

LARIX

Larch

Conifer

A tall tree for parkland and not the average garden. One of the few deciduous conifers — there are bare knobbly branches in winter. In spring tufts of needle-like leaves appear.

L. decidua

VARIETIES   Ⓓ

L. decidua – 5 m; 25 m or more when mature. Common Larch. Graceful with downswept branches. Yellow leaves in autumn. Oval cones turn brown with age.

L. kaempferi – 5 m; 25 m or more when mature. Japanese Larch. Similar to above but leaves are grey-green and not bright green.

SITE & SOIL
11

PROPAGATION
5

FLOWER TIME
—

PRUNING
1

LAURUS

L. nobilis

Bay Laurel

Tree
● Shrub

The place for Bay Laurel is in the herb garden or neatly trimmed in a container. Do not confuse with the more popular laurel (Prunus lusitanica) which is used for hedging.

VARIETIES   Ⓔ

L. nobilis – 2.5 m; usually kept in check by annual pruning. Sweet Bay. Tiny yellow spring flowers followed by black berries may appear on untrained female trees. Glossy oval leaves have wavy edges — may be damaged by frosts. Choose a sheltered site.

L. n. 'Aurea' – Yellow leaves.

L. nobilis

SITE & SOIL
10

PROPAGATION
5

FLOWER TIME
—

PRUNING	
13	Spring and summer

LAVANDULA

L. stoechas

Lavender

Shrub

A popular low-growing bush for the front of the border or for dwarf hedging. The aromatic flowers and stalks have been used for making pot-pourri for centuries.

VARIETIES   Ⓔ

L. angustifolia (L. spica) – 75 cm. Pale blue. Old English Lavender.

L. a. 'Hidcote' – 45 cm. Purple.

L. a. 'Nana Alba' – 30 cm. White.

L. a. 'Munstead' – 45 cm. Lavender.

L. stoechas – 40 cm. Purple. French Lavender. Showy flowers.

L. viridis – 40 cm. White. Green leaves.

L. angustifolia 'Hidcote'

SITE & SOIL
2

PROPAGATION
1

FLOWER TIME
July — September

PRUNING	
23	April

LAVATERA

L. 'Burgundy Wine'
Tree Mallow

Shrub

A good choice if you want a quick-growing shrub which will produce large flowers all summer long, but you must remember to hard prune it every year.

VARIETIES (SE)

L. 'Rosea' – 2 m. Pink. Large leaves.
L. 'Barnsley' – 2 m. Red-eyed pinkish-white. Popular.
L. 'Burgundy Wine' – 1.5 m. Pink.
L. 'Ice Cool' – 1.2 m. White.
L. 'Pink Frills' – 1.2 m. Pink. Small flowers.
L. maritima – 1.5 m. Purple-veined lilac. Not fully hardy.

L. 'Rosea'

SITE & SOIL
2

PROPAGATION
3

FLOWER TIME
June — October

PRUNING
11   April

LEPTOSPERMUM

L. scoparium
New Zealand Tea Tree

Shrub

Well worth growing, but only if the conditions are right. It needs a mild climate or the protection of a south-facing wall. The saucer-shaped blooms are long-lasting.

VARIETIES (E)

L. scoparium – 2.5 m. White. A variety is the usual choice:
L. s. 'Red Damask' – Red. Double. Purple-tinged leaves.
L. s. 'Snow Flurry' – White. Double.
L. s. 'Kiwi' – Red. Single. Dwarf.
L. s. 'Nichollsii' – Rose-pink. Single.
L. lanigerum – White. Hardier than L. scoparium varieties. Compact.

L. scoparium 'Nichollsii'

SITE & SOIL
9

PROPAGATION
1

FLOWER TIME
May — June

PRUNING
2   Early spring

LESPEDEZA

L. thunbergii
Bush Clover

Shrub

Arching stems with long flower trusses in late summer make it sound desirable for the border, but there are drawbacks. Growth is untidy and leaves appear late.

VARIETIES (D)

L. thunbergii – 1.2 m. Rosy-purple. Pea-like flowers. Foliage appears in early summer. Yellow leaves in autumn. Wide-spreading growth. Branches may die down in winter. Poor in heavy soil.
L. t. 'Albiflora' – White.
L. bicolor – 3 m. Purple/pink. Semi-erect growth habit.

L. thunbergii

SITE & SOIL
20

PROPAGATION
1

FLOWER TIME
August — October

PRUNING
18

LEUCOTHOE

L. 'Scarletta'
Leucothoe

Shrub

Attractive ground cover with year-round interest for acid soil and a shady situation. All are attractively coloured in winter and one bears flowers in late spring.

L. fontanesiana

VARIETIES Ⓔ or ⓈⒺ

L. fontanesiana – 1 m. White. Lance-shaped leaves — green, turning bronzy-purple in winter.
L. f. 'Rainbow' – 1 m. White. Pendent flowers. Green/yellow/pink/cream variegated leaves.
L. 'Scarletta' – 30 cm. Leaves red at first, then purple to green and finally bronze.

SITE & SOIL
6

PROPAGATION
1/6

FLOWER TIME
May

PRUNING
8   Spring

LEYCESTERIA

L. formosa
Pheasant Berry

Shrub

Gaunt in winter — a thicket of wax-coated bamboo-like stems. Severe frost may kill some shoots. In summer there are flower tassels followed by berries in autumn.

L. formosa

VARIETIES Ⓓ

L. formosa – 2 m. White/reddish-purple. Tassels made up of small flowers within showy bracts. Purple berries much loved by birds are borne within the bracts. Quick-growing. Remove dead stems in spring.
L. crocothyrsos – 2 m. Yellow. Summer-flowering. Green berries.

SITE & SOIL
10

PROPAGATION
1

FLOWER TIME
June — September

PRUNING
8   March

LIGUSTRUM

L. ovalifolium 'Aureum'
Hedging Privet

Shrub

Privet is no longer the first choice for urban hedging. Its resistance to smoky air is not needed any more, but some of the colourful varieties are useful in poor situations.

L. ovalifolium 'Argenteum'

VARIETIES ⓈⒺ

L. vulgare – 3 m if left untrimmed. Common Privet. All-green leaves.
L. ovalifolium – 2 m if left untrimmed. Oval-leaf Privet. Glossy leaves — larger than above.
L. o. 'Aureum' – Golden Privet. Green-centred yellow leaves.
L. o. 'Argenteum' – Cream-edged green leaves.

SITE & SOIL
16

PROPAGATION
3

FLOWER TIME
—

PRUNING
24

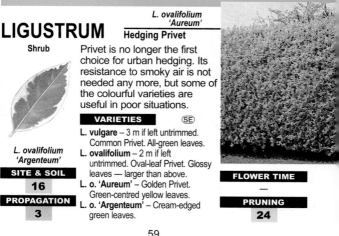

LIGUSTRUM

Shrub

L. japonicum
Flowering Privet

Privet has long been regarded as a grow-anywhere hedging plant with dull leaves and even less interesting flowers. There are, however, several species with large flower-heads.

L. sinense

VARIETIES Ⓓ or Ⓔ

L. quihoui – 2.5 m. White. August-September. Deciduous. 30 cm long flower-heads.

L. japonicum – 1.5 m. White. July-September. Evergreen.

L. lucidum – 4.5 m. White. August-September. Evergreen.

L. sinense – 4.5 m. White. July. Evergreen.

SITE & SOIL
10

PROPAGATION
3

FLOWER TIME
Depends on species

PRUNING
2 Spring

LIQUIDAMBAR

Tree

L. styraciflua
Sweet Gum

The leaves are maple-like but they are arranged alternately on the branches. The bark is attractive but the main feature is the brightly-coloured autumn foliage.

L. styraciflua

VARIETIES Ⓓ

L. styraciflua – 5 m. 15 cm long lobed leaves. Leaves turn orange and reddish-purple in autumn — colour is heightened in moist and acid soil. Corky bark.

L. s. 'Variegata' – White-edged leaves.

L. s. 'Worpleston' – Red leaves in autumn.

SITE & SOIL
7

PROPAGATION
5

FLOWER TIME
—

PRUNING
2 Spring

LIRIODENDRON

Tree

L. tulipifera
Tulip Tree

A tree with uniquely-shaped leaves — 4-lobed with a flattened tip. At the end of the season the foliage turns bright gold. Flowers do not appear for about 25 years.

L. tulipifera

VARIETIES Ⓓ

L. tulipifera – 8 m. Green/yellow/pink tulip-like flowers. A specimen tree for parkland and estate gardens — for smaller gardens choose a variety:

L. t. 'Aureomarginatum' – 4 m. Yellow-edged green leaves.

L. t. 'Fastigiatum' – 6 m. Pillar-like growth habit.

SITE & SOIL
11

PROPAGATION
5

FLOWER TIME
June — July

PRUNING
2 Spring

LONICERA

Climber

L. periclymenum 'Serotina'

Climbing Honeysuckle

Less demanding than Clematis. It will grow in sun or light shade and produce masses of colourful blooms, but it is an untidy plant which needs to ramble.

L. periclymenum

VARIETIES	Ⓓ or ⓈⒺ

L. periclymenum – 6 m. Cream/red. Woodbine. July-August.
L. p. 'Belgica' – Blooms early.
L. p. 'Serotina' – Blooms late.
L. americana – 7 m. Yellow/rose. June-September.
L. japonica 'Aureoreticulata' – 3.5 m. Yellow. July-August. Yellow-netted green leaves.

SITE & SOIL
7

PROPAGATION
1/6

FLOWER TIME
Depends on species

PRUNING
25 After flowering

LONICERA

Shrub

L. nitida 'Baggesen's Gold'

Shrubby Honeysuckle

Not all honeysuckles are climbers. There are non-flowering ones for hedging and for use as ground cover and also flowering bushy types for the border.

L. tatarica

VARIETIES	Ⓓ or ⓈⒺ or Ⓔ

L. nitida – 2 m. Tiny leaves. Often used as hedging. Evergreen.
L. n. 'Baggesen's Gold' – Yellow leaves.
L. pileata – 60 cm. Shiny berries. Use as ground cover.
L. tatarica – 3 m. Pink. June.
L. fragrantissima – 3 m. Cream. January-March. Red berries.

SITE & SOIL
7

PROPAGATION
1/6

FLOWER TIME
Depends on species

PRUNING
24 or 10 After flowering

LUPINUS

Shrub

L. arboreus

Tree Lupin

Unlike its herbaceous border cousin, the Tree Lupin is a rarity. It is short-lived, and the floral spikes are shorter than the heads on hardy perennial hybrids.

L. arboreus

VARIETIES	ⓈⒺ or Ⓔ

L. arboreus – 1.5 m. Yellow. Fragrant flowers. Greyish-green leaflets. 1.5 m spread — sprawling growth habit. Thrives in poor sandy soil and coastal areas — do not plant in heavy soil.
L. a. 'Mauve Queen' – Pale purple.
L. albifrons – 80 cm. Blue/white. 20 cm long flower spikes.

SITE & SOIL
20

PROPAGATION
1/12

FLOWER TIME
June — August

PRUNING
13 March

LYCIUM

Shrub

L. barbarum

Lycium

An untidy plant which is not recommended for the border. It thrives in the sandy soil and salt-laden air near the coast — use it there for hedging or covering a bank.

VARIETIES Ⓓ

L. barbarum – 2 m. Lilac. Duke of Argyll's Tea Tree. Funnel-shaped flowers. Short, strap-like leaves. 3-4 m spread — arching growth habit. Fast-growing and fully hardy. Flowers are followed by 3 cm long orange or red egg-shaped berries. Rare — in some catalogues but not the garden centre.

SITE & SOIL
20

PROPAGATION
1

FLOWER TIME
June — September

PRUNING
8   March

MAGNOLIA

Shrub

M. stellata

M. soulangiana 'Alba Superba'

M. soulangiana 'Rustica Rubra'

M. grandiflora

SITE & SOIL
9

PROPAGATION
5

Magnolia

A mature Magnolia in full bloom is a splendid sight, but there are a few rules you will have to follow to ensure success. Plant in April (not autumn) and give the bush plenty of room to spread. Choose a spot away from a frost pocket and provide shelter from northerly and easterly winds. Add organic matter to the soil and don't plant too deeply. Water the bush copiously during the first season if the weather is dry and do not hoe close to the plant stems. Mulch with a layer of compost in spring.

VARIETIES Ⓓ or Ⓔ

M. stellata – 1.2 m. White. Star Magnolia. March-April.
M. s. 'Royal Star' – Larger flowers. April-May.
M. lilliflora 'Nigra' – 1.5 m. Purple/white. May.
M. loebneri 'Leonard Messel' – 1.5 m. Lilac-pink/white. May.
M. soulangiana – 3 m. Pink/white. April-May.
M. s. 'Alba Superba' – 1.2 m. All-white.
M. s. 'Rustica Rubra' – 1.2 m. All-pink.
M. grandiflora – 3.5 m. Creamy-white. July-September. Evergreen. Flowers first appear after 20-25 years.

M. stellata

M. soulangiana

FLOWER TIME
Depends on species

PRUNING
2   After flowering

MAHONIA

Mahonia

Shrub

M. aquifolium

M. japonica

M. media 'Charity'

A popular provider of year-round colour. Green, glossy leaves which are sometimes tinged with purple in winter, fragrant flowers in winter or spring and then purple or black berries. All of the popular Mahonias are hardy and easy to grow — they are not fussy about soil type and will grow in shade. Use them as ground cover under trees or close to the north side of the house. In the catalogues you will find some unusual species listed — choose with care as some of these choice ones are rather tender.

VARIETIES   Ⓔ

M. aquifolium – 1 m. Yellow. March-April. Oregon Grape.
M. a. 'Apollo' – Non-invasive variety.
M. a. 'Atropurpurea' – Purple winter leaves.
M. japonica – 2 m. Yellow. November-February. Flower spikes radiate from stem tips.
M. j. 'Bealei' – Short flower spikes.
M. media – 2 m. Popular hybrids with spoke-like flower-heads. November-February.
M. m. 'Charity' – Popular specimen shrub.
M. m. 'Lionel Fortesque' – Very long spikes.
M. lomarifolia – 2.5 m. November-February. Rather tender.

M. aquifolium 'Atropurpurea'

M. lomarifolia

SITE & SOIL
15

PROPAGATION
1

FLOWER TIME
Depends on species

PRUNING
2   April

MALUS

M. 'Profusion'

Ornamental Crab

Tree

M. 'Golden Hornet'

Prunus is the favourite spring-flowering tree, but Malus has some extra points. There are red as well as white and pink varieties, fruits are often large and it tolerates heavy soil.

VARIETIES   Ⓓ

M. 'John Downie' – 6 m. White. Orange/scarlet fruits. Popular.
M. 'Golden Hornet' – 6 m. White. Yellow long-lasting fruits. Popular.
M. floribunda – 5 m. Pink, turning white. Arching. Yellow fruits.
M. 'Profusion' – 6 m. Red, turning pink. Coppery leaves. Small red fruits.

SITE & SOIL
2

PROPAGATION
5

FLOWER TIME
April — May

PRUNING
2   Winter

METASEQUOIA

Conifer

This conifer, known only from fossils, was discovered in China in 1941. It is a quick-growing tree which loses its leaves in winter. Closely related to Taxodium.

VARIETIES Ⓓ

M. glyptostroboides – 5 m; mature height not known but expected to be over 35 m. Feathery foliage, pale green in summer changing to pink/gold in autumn. 3 cm long round pendulous cones. Shaggy bark. Grow a young specimen for interest, but an adult tree will need to be in parkland.

M. glyptostroboides

SITE & SOIL
7

PROPAGATION
5

FLOWER TIME
—

PRUNING
1

MORUS

M. alba 'Pendula'

Mulberry

Tree

The gnarled trunk and orange scaly bark of Black Mulberry are interesting features in winter and in late summer the edible blackberry-like fruits appear on mature trees.

VARIETIES Ⓓ

M. nigra – 3 m; 8 m when mature. Black Mulberry. Large, heart-shaped leaves. Red berries change to purple when ripe.

M. nigra

SITE & SOIL
10

M. alba – 4 m; 12 m when mature. White Mulberry. Tasteless pink or black berries in autumn.

PROPAGATION
3

M. a. 'Pendula' – 3 m. Black berries. Pendulous branches.

BERRY TIME
August — September

PRUNING
1

MYRICA

M. gale

Bayberry

Shrub

A small group of unusual and unspectacular acid-loving plants — the soil must be either very moist or dry and starved depending on the species you choose.

VARIETIES Ⓓ or Ⓔ

M. gale – 1.5 m; 3 m when mature. Brown. Bog Myrtle. Catkins on female plants in April-May, followed by small brown berries. Needs boggy land. Deciduous.

M. pennsylvanica

SITE & SOIL
Depends on species

M. californica – 3 m. Evergreen.

PROPAGATION
1

M. pennsylvanica – 2 m; 5 m when mature. Purplish-white berries. Needs poor dry soil. Deciduous.

BERRY TIME
November — January

PRUNING
1

MYRTUS

Shrub

M. communis

SITE & SOIL
2

PROPAGATION
2

M. communis

Myrtle

Myrtle has been one of our garden shrubs for hundreds of years, but it is not a popular plant. The problem is that it is damaged by hard frosts and icy winds.

VARIETIES Ⓔ

M. communis – 3 m. White. Small flowers with a central boss of fluffy stamens. Black berries.

M. c. 'Tarentina' – 1 m. White.

M. c. 'Variegata' – 2 m. White. Cream-edged leaves. Rather tender.

M. luma (Luma apiculata) – 6 m. White. Dull leaves. Purple berries.

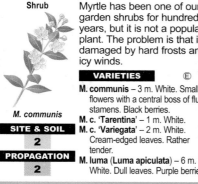

FLOWER TIME
July — September

PRUNING
2 Late spring

NANDINA

Shrub

N. domestica

SITE & SOIL
2

PROPAGATION
10

N. domestica 'Firepower'

Heavenly Bamboo

Colours change as the year progresses. Spring foliage is tinged with red and in autumn the green leaves are flushed with purple. White flowers are followed by berries.

VARIETIES Ⓔ

N. domestica – 1.2 m. White. Cone-shaped flower-heads bear 1 cm wide starry blooms. Leaves made up of oval leaflets — may fall in winter. Upright stems are unbranched.

N. d. 'Firepower' – 0.6 m. White. More compact and more colourful than the species.

FLOWER TIME
June — July

PRUNING
5 Early spring

NEILLIA

Shrub

N. longiracemosa

SITE & SOIL
10

PROPAGATION
1

N. longiracemosa

Neillia

A graceful shrub with slender upright branches. It steadily spreads to form a thicket and in early summer pendent flower sprays appear. Easy to grow but not often seen.

VARIETIES Ⓓ

N. longiracemosa – 2 m. Pink. 8-15 cm long sprays of 20-30 tubular flowers. Saw-edged leaves have prominent veins. Downy stems. Most widely available species.

N. affinis – 2 m. Pink. 5-8 cm long flower sprays.

N. sinensis – 3 m. White. 5 cm long flower sprays.

FLOWER TIME
May — June

PRUNING
10 After flowering

NOTHOFAGUS

N. antarctica
Antarctic Beech

Tree

An attractive tree for parkland or large gardens, but it is more demanding than its better-known relative, the Common Beech. It dislikes alkaline soil and strong winds.

VARIETIES Ⓓ or Ⓔ

N. antarctica – 8 m. 3 cm long leaves are glossy and saw-edged. Fruits look like small beech masts. Yellow leaves in autumn. Quick-growing. The most popular species. Deciduous.

N. obliqua – 8 m. Good autumn colour. Deciduous.

N. dombeyi – 8 m. Evergreen.

N. antarctica

SITE & SOIL
9

PROPAGATION
5

FLOWER TIME
—

PRUNING
2 Winter

NYSSA

N. sylvatica
Tupelo

Tree

Quite an ordinary tree for most of the year — the flowers are inconspicuous and the berries are small. It is in autumn that the tree stands out with its brilliant leaf colouring.

VARIETIES Ⓓ

N. sylvatica – 4 m; 10 m when mature. Tiny green flowers on slender shoots open in summer — autumn berries are quickly removed by birds. 10 cm long glossy oval leaves turn golden and then red in autumn. Slow-growing.

N. sinensis – 3 m; 8 m when mature. Young leaves are red.

N. sylvatica

SITE & SOIL
14

PROPAGATION
5

BERRY TIME
September — October

PRUNING
2 Autumn

OLEARIA

O. haastii
Daisy Bush

Shrub

The bush is covered with small daisy-like flowers in summer, but it can become gaunt and unattractive when not in flower if it is not pruned annually.

VARIETIES Ⓔ

O. macrodonta – 2.4 m. White. June-July. Holly-like leaves are sage green above, silver-felted below.

O. haastii – 1.8 m. White. July-August. Box-like leaves.

O. scilloniensis – 1.5 m. White. May. Less hardy than species above.

O. scilloniensis

SITE & SOIL
2

PROPAGATION
1

FLOWER TIME
Depends on species

PRUNING
8 After flowering

OSMANTHUS

O. heterophyllus 'Variegatus'

Osmanthus

Shrub

A neat and rounded bush densely covered with evergreen leaves. The small flowers have a jasmine-like fragrance. Use it in the border or for hedging.

VARIETIES Ⓔ

O. delavayi – 1.2 m. White. April-May. Tubular flowers are plentiful. The most popular species.

O. burkwoodii – 2 m. White. April-May. Similar to above but more vigorous — suitable for hedging.

O. heterophyllus 'Variegatus' – 1.5 m. White. September. Cream-edged holly-like leaves.

O. burkwoodii

SITE & SOIL
3

PROPAGATION
1

FLOWER TIME
Depends on species

PRUNING
2   After flowering

OZOTHAMNUS

O. ledifolius

Ozothamnus

Shrub

A close relative of Helichrysum — both produce 'everlasting' flowers. Unlike Helichrysum the buds are brown and the white flowers have red or brown bracts.

VARIETIES Ⓔ

O. ledifolius – 1 m. White. 5 cm wide flower clusters — seed heads have a honey-like fragrance. The gum on the leaves and stems is inflammable — hence the common name Kerosene Bush.

O. rosmarinifolius – 1.5 m. White. Rosemary-like foliage. Young stems covered with white wool.

O. rosmarinifolius

SITE & SOIL
20

PROPAGATION
1

FLOWER TIME
June — August

PRUNING
2   Spring

PACHYSANDRA

P. terminalis

Japanese Spurge

Shrub

Useful for growing in the shade under trees. It is low growing and the densely-packed leathery leaves suppress weed growth. Does not flourish in chalky soil.

VARIETIES Ⓔ

P. terminalis – 20 cm. White. Tiny white blooms on short stalks have little decorative value. 10 cm long glossy leaves are borne in clusters. Excellent ground cover.

P. t. 'Green Carpet' – 10 cm. White. More compact than the species.

P. t. 'Variegata' – 20 cm. White. Cream-edged green leaves.

P. terminalis 'Variegata'

SITE & SOIL
17

PROPAGATION
10

FLOWER TIME
March

PRUNING
13   Summer

PAEONIA

P. lemoinei

Tree Peony

Shrub

Tree Peonies are less popular than their herbaceous border relatives. Flowers are large bowls or balls of papery petals. Double blooms need staking.

VARIETIES ⓓ

P. suffruticosa varieties – 2 m. White, pink or red. Large cup-shaped flowers.

P. delavayi

P. delavayi – 1.5 m. Red. Single. Ornamental leaves. Popular.

SITE & SOIL
22

P. lutea ludlowii – 1.8 m. Yellow Single. Popular.

PROPAGATION
5

P. lemoinei – 2 m. Yellow. Large cup-shaped flowers.

FLOWER TIME
May — June

PRUNING
2   Early summer

PARAHEBE

P. catarractae

Parahebe

Shrub

Use Parahebe for ground cover or as a specimen plant in the rockery. Reputed to be tender but the species listed below are reasonably hardy. Blooms are borne in clusters.

VARIETIES ⓔ

P. catarractae – 30 cm. Red-eyed, purple-veined white or mauve. Small saw-edged leaves.

P. catarractae

P. c. 'Diffusa' – 15 cm. Red-eyed pink-veined white.

SITE & SOIL
2

P. hookeriana – 15 cm. Red-eyed white or mauve.

PROPAGATION
1

P. bidwillii 'Kea' – 10 cm. Red-veined white. Prostrate.

FLOWER TIME
July — September

PRUNING
2   Spring

PARTHENOCISSUS

P. quinquefolia

Virginia Creeper

Climber

Spreading vines frequently used to clothe house walls. They need some support at first, but unlike Vitis soon become self-clinging. The leaves turn red in autumn.

VARIETIES ⓓ

P. tricuspidata 'Veitchii' – 7 m. Boston Ivy. Leaf shape variable — usually 3-lobed.

P. tricuspidata

P. quinquefolia – 7 m. Dull green — 5-lobed leaves.

SITE & SOIL
4

P. henryana – 5 m. Chinese Virginia Creeper. White-veined green marked with red — 3- or 5-lobed leaves.

PROPAGATION
6

FLOWER TIME
—

PRUNING
2   Early spring

PASSIFLORA

Climber

P. caerulea

P. caerulea
Passion Flower

Very few can be grown out-doors, and even the hardiest must be grown against a south- or west-facing wall. Frost may cut down stems — new ones appear.

VARIETIES ⒹorⓈⒺ

P. caerulea – 7 m. White/purple/blue. Intricate 8 cm wide flowers with prominent stamens, styles and stigmas. Large leaves with 5 or 7 lobes. Stout support needed for tendrils. After a hot summer orange egg-shaped fruits appear in autumn.

P. c. 'Constance Elliott' – 7 m. White.

SITE & SOIL
1

PROPAGATION
1

FLOWER TIME
July — September

PRUNING
2 April

PAULOWNIA

Tree

P. tomentosa

P. tomentosa
Paulownia

There are giant leaves and erect spikes of foxglove-like flowers providing an exotic effect, but patience and good weather are necessary for this display.

VARIETIES Ⓓ

P. tomentosa – 7 m; 14 m when mature. Mauve. 30 cm high spikes with 5 cm long flowers. Grey-green 25 cm wide leaves. Flower buds appear in autumn after a fine summer — a mild winter ensures a good spring display. Blooms do not appear for many years after planting.

SITE & SOIL
1

PROPAGATION
5

FLOWER TIME
May

PRUNING
2 Early spring

PERNETTYA

Shrub

P. mucronata
'Alba'

P. mucronata
'Cherry Ripe'
Prickly Heath

A low-growing prickly bush with showy berries which the birds leave alone. Masses of early summer flowers are followed by large porcelain-like fruits on female plants.

VARIETIES Ⓔ

P. mucronata – 80 cm. Creamy-white. 2 cm long dark green leaves.
P. m. 'Thymifolia' – Male.
P. m. 'Mascula' – Male.
P. m. 'Alba' – White berries.
P. m. 'Cherry Ripe' – Red berries.
P. m. 'Lilian' – Pink berries.
P. m. 'Bell's Seedling' – Dark pink berries Male/Female.

SITE & SOIL
18

PROPAGATION
8

BERRY TIME
November — February

PRUNING
2 Spring

PEROVSKIA

Shrub

P. atriplicifolia

P. atriplicifolia
'Blue Spire'
Russian Sage

Like lavender there are tiny blue flowers on long spikes above stiff erect stems and grey leaves. Unlike lavender foliage is deeply cut or toothed and it has a sage-like smell.

VARIETIES ⓓ

P. atriplicifolia – 1 m. Lavender. 25 cm long flower spikes. Use to provide a haze of end-of-season colour in the border. A late starter which is hard-pruned, so there is little to see in spring and early summer.

P. a. 'Blue Spire' – More attractive than the species.

SITE & SOIL
1

PROPAGATION
1

FLOWER TIME
August — October

PRUNING
11 April

PHILADELPHUS

Shrub

P. 'Virginal'

P. coronarius

Mock Orange

Philadelphus provides abundant blooms in the high-summer gap between the spring floral display in the garden and the bright leaf colours of autumn. The usual height is about 2 m, but there are taller varieties as well as dwarfs. The blooms have an orange-blossom fragrance and the shrub will grow almost anywhere, but it does need some sun and you must prune it properly every year. The flowering period lasts for only a few weeks and blackfly can be a problem. Sometimes wrongly referred to as Syringa.

P. 'Erectus'

VARIETIES ⓓ

Tall varieties (over 3 m):
  P. 'Virginal' – White. Double.
  P. coronarius – Creamy-white. Spreading.
Medium varieties (1.5-3 m):
  P. coronarius 'Aureus' – White. Yellow leaves.
  P. 'Beauclerk' – Pink-flushed white.
  P. 'Belle Etoile' – Pink-flushed white. Frilled petals. Semi-arching.
  P. 'Erectus' – White. Small strongly-scented flowers. Erect.
Small varieties (under 1.5 m):
  P. 'Sybille' – 1 m. Pink-flushed white.
  P. 'Manteau d'Hermine' – 80 cm. Creamy-white. Double.

P. 'Sybille'

P. coronarius 'Aureus'

SITE & SOIL
11

PROPAGATION
1/3

FLOWER TIME
June — July

PRUNING
8 After flowering

PHILLYREA

Phillyrea

P. decora

Shrub

Grown in the border or woodland to provide a year-round display of strap-shaped or oval leaves on rounded bushes. The floral display is insignificant.

VARIETIES Ⓔ

P. latifolia

P. angustifolia – 3 m. Greenish-white. 1 cm wide clusters of tiny blooms. Blue-black berries.
P. latifolia – 5 m. Greenish-white. 8 cm long oval glossy leaves.
P. decora – 3 m. White. Tubular flowers larger and showier than above. Now renamed **Osmanthus decorus**.

SITE & SOIL
2

PROPAGATION
1

FLOWER TIME
May — June

PRUNING
2   After flowering

PHLOMIS

Jerusalem Sage

P. fruticosa

Shrub

Easy to recognise — whorls of hooded flowers are borne on the top of woolly-leaved stems. Plants become unattractive with age — hard prune every year to ensure new stems.

VARIETIES Ⓔ

P. fruticosa

P. fruticosa – 1 m. Yellow. 5 cm wide flower whorls. Furry grey-green leaves. Spreading growth habit. Good drought resistance.
P. chrysophylla – Similar to P. fruticosa, but leaves turn yellow in late summer.
P. italica – 60 cm. Lilac. Flowers on terminal spikes.

SITE & SOIL
2

PROPAGATION
1

FLOWER TIME
June — July

PRUNING
11   Spring

PHORMIUM

New Zealand Flax

P. tenax 'Purpureum'

Shrub

An architectural plant with sword-like leaves — use it where you want a tropical touch in green, yellow, bronze or purple. No stems — just a bold clump of leaves.

VARIETIES Ⓔ

P. cookianum 'Cream Delight'

P. tenax – 1-1.5 m. Red. Small flowers on long stalks.
P. t. 'Purpureum' – Purple leaves.
P. 'Sundowner' – Pink leaves.
P. 'Yellow Wave' – Yellow leaves.
P. 'Bronze Baby' – Coppery leaves.
P. cookianum – 60 cm. Yellow.
P. c. 'Cream Delight' – Green-edged cream leaves.

SITE & SOIL
1

PROPAGATION
10

FLOWER TIME
July

PRUNING
2   Spring

PHOTINIA

Shrub

P. fraseri 'Robusta'

P. fraseri 'Red Robin'
Photinia

'Red Robin' has become a firm favourite in recent years. The young foliage in spring is bright red — cut back once this colour has faded and new red leaves will appear.

VARIETIES (E)

P. fraseri 'Red Robin' – 2.5 m. White. Clusters of small flowers appear after a mild winter. Oval dark green leaves, new growth fiery red like Pieris but Photinia will grow in alkaline soil. Plant in a sheltered spot.

P. f. 'Robusta' – 3 m. Coppery young growth.

SITE & SOIL
11

PROPAGATION
2

FLOWER TIME
April

PRUNING
2 Early spring

PHYGELIUS

Shrub

P. capensis

P. aequalis 'Yellow Trumpet'
Cape Figwort

Eye-catching flower-heads — worth trying against a wall if your garden is in a mild area. In spring cut off all stems or just trim off frost-affected side shoots.

VARIETIES (SE) or (E)

P. aequalis 'Yellow Trumpet' – 1 m. Yellow. Tubular blooms on one-sided flower-heads.

P. capensis – 2.5 m. Yellow-throated red. Flowers all round the spike.

P. rectus has numerous varieties — e.g **'African Queen'** (Red), **'Salmon Leap'** (Orange) and **'Winchester Fanfare'** (Pink).

SITE & SOIL
3

PROPAGATION
2

FLOWER TIME
July — October

PRUNING
18 or **2** April

PHYSOCARPUS

Shrub

P. opulifolius 'Luteus'

P. opulifolius 'Dart's Gold'
Nine Bark

Colourful — yellow leaves, white flowers, red fruits and coloured wood under bark which peels in winter. No problems, but midday sun may scorch leaves.

VARIETIES (D)

P. opulifolius – 3 m. White. Ball-like flower clusters. 3-lobed green leaves. Varieties are preferred.

P. o. 'Luteus' – 2.5 m. White. Yellow leaves.

P. o. 'Dart's Gold' – 2 m. White. An improvement on 'Luteus'.

P. o. 'Diabolo' – 2 m. White. Dark bronze leaves.

SITE & SOIL
5

PROPAGATION
1/3

FLOWER TIME
June — July

PRUNING
8 After flowering

PICEA

Conifer

Spruce

The typical Picea has a Christmas tree shape with examples as low as a metre or as high as 50 m. These species can be mistaken for Abies, but the leaf base on a Picea branch is a raised peg and not a sunken scar. Not all Piceas are conical — there are weeping trees and squat bushes. The leaves are more needle-like than strap-shaped and the oval or cylindrical cones hang downwards. Nearly all will thrive in cold and wet soils, but some are not tolerant of poor growing conditions when young.

P. omorika

P. glauca 'Albertiana Conica'

VARIETIES (E)

P. abies – 3.5 m. Norway Spruce. Usually sold as Christmas trees. Not a good garden tree.
P. a. 'Nidiformis' – 30 cm. Flat-topped — horizontal branches in layers.
P. breweriana – 2 m; 12 m when mature. Broadly conical and weeping — branches bear pendulous branchlets.
P. glauca 'Albertiana Conica' – 60 cm; 2 m when mature. Neat cone. Popular rockery conifer.
P. omorika – 3.5 m. Serbian Spruce. Narrowly conical. Branches curve upwards at the tips.
P. pungens – Blue Spruce. A variety is usually chosen.
P. p. 'Koster' – 2 m; 8 m when mature. Silvery blue.
P. p. 'Hoopsii' – 2 m. Conical.
P. p. 'Globosa' – 60 cm. Round.
P. mariana 'Nana' – 30 cm. Black Spruce. Dwarf. Tight ball of foliage.
P. orientalis 'Aurea' – 3.5 m. Foliage yellow in spring.

SITE & SOIL
11

PROPAGATION
5

P. pungens 'Globosa'

FLOWER TIME
—

PRUNING	
2	Spring

PIERIS

Shrub

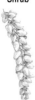

P. japonica

P. formosa forrestii 'Wakehurst'

Andromeda

In spring there are long sprays of bell-shaped blooms and with the more popular varieties there is a bright red display of young foliage. Neat and slow-growing.

VARIETIES (E)

P. formosa forrestii – 3 m. White. Foliage red when young. **'Wakehurst'** (Bright red leaves), **'Jermyns'** (Red flower buds).
P. japonica – 2 m. White or pink. Early flowering. Varieties include **'Valley Valentine'** (Red flowers).
P. 'Forest Flame' – Red/cream/green leaves.

SITE & SOIL
14

PROPAGATION
6

FLOWER TIME
March — May

PRUNING	
2	Late winter

PILEOSTEGIA

Climber

P. viburnoides

SITE & SOIL

4

PROPAGATION

1/6

P. viburnoides
Pileostegia

This plant is not fully hardy nor is it particularly showy. It is included here because evergreen flowering climbers which will thrive in shade are rare.

VARIETIES Ⓔ

P. viburnoides – 6 m. Creamy white. Masses of tiny flowers in 10-15 cm wide clusters. 15 cm long lance-shaped dark green leaves. Closely related to Hydrangea. Like H. petiolaris it has aerial roots which attach the plant to the support and it will thrive on a north-facing wall. Slow growing.

FLOWER TIME
August — October

PRUNING

2   Late winter

PINUS

Conifer

P. sylvestris

Pine

Most pines are far too tall for the average garden, but there are slow-growing ones and dwarfs which are suitable for the border or rockery. The long needles borne in bundles of two to five make a welcome change from the scale-like or strap-shaped leaves of the more popular conifers. Young growth often forms a candle-like structure. Cones are oval and remain on the tree for several years. Sandy soil is not a problem nor is exposure to strong winds, but pines suffer on a shady site or in polluted air.

P. sylvestris

VARIETIES Ⓔ

P. sylvestris – 4 m; 20 m or more when mature. Scots Pine. Twisted grey-green needles borne in pairs. Red bark. Slow-growing varieties for the garden include **'Aurea'** (Yellow winter foliage), **'Beuvronensis'** (Dome-shaped rockery variety) and **'Fastigiata'** (Narrow column-shaped).

P. nigra – 3 m. Austrian Pine. Good specimen tree. Dwarf variety is **'Hornibrookiana'**.

P. strobus 'Nana' – 60 cm. Dwarf form of Weymouth Pine. Spreading. Silvery blue-green.

P. wallichiana – 3 m. Bhutan Pine. Attractive — lower branches retained. Young foliage bluish-green.

P. mugo – 60 cm. Mountain Pine. Leaves in pairs. Popular dwarf.

P. m. 'Gnom' – 60 cm. Compact mound. Dark green leaves.

P. aristata – 2 m. Bristlecone Pine. Resin-flecked leaves.

P. strobus 'Nana'

SITE & SOIL

1

PROPAGATION

5

FLOWER TIME
—

PRUNING

1

PIPTANTHUS

P. laburnifolius
Evergreen Laburnum

Shrub

Like Laburnum there are flower-heads of yellow pea-like flowers. Unlike Laburnum it is semi-evergreen, rather tender and the flower-heads are erect.

VARIETIES (SE)

P. laburnifolius (P. nepalensis) – 3 m. Yellow. 4 cm long flowers, followed by grey pods in autumn. Each leaf has three 10 cm long dark green glossy leaflets. Grow it against a south- or west-facing wall. Good drought resistance, but it is not a long-lived plant. Not easy to find.

P. laburnifolius

SITE & SOIL
2

PROPAGATION
1

FLOWER TIME
May — June

PRUNING	
2	Spring

PITTOSPORUM

P. tobira
Pittosporum

Shrub

The black twigs with their wavy-edged leaves are popular with flower arrangers, but part or all of the bush may die in a severe winter. Few types offer a floral display.

VARIETIES (E)

P. tenuifolium – 3 m. Purple. Small flowers may appear. Grey-green leaves. Reasonably hardy.

P. t. 'Limelight' – 3 m. Dark green/ pale green leaves.

P. 'Garnettii' – 2 m. White-edged grey-green leaves.

P. tobira – 3 m. White. Best flowering type, but tender.

P. tenuifolium

SITE & SOIL
3

PROPAGATION
1

FLOWER TIME
May

PRUNING	
2	Spring

PLATANUS

P. hispanica
Plane

Tree

For nearly everyone this is a tree to admire and not to grow — it would overwhelm the average garden. Easily recognised by the creamy patches beneath the flaking bark.

VARIETIES (D)

P. hispanica (P. acerifolia) – 10 m; 20 m when mature. London Plane. Broadly-domed fast-growing tree — thrives in urban situations. 5-lobed maple-like leaves. Ball-shaped seed pods in winter.

P. orientalis – 10 m. More spreading than London Plane. Leaves more deeply cut to form narrow lobes.

P. hispanica

SITE & SOIL
10

PROPAGATION
1

FLOWER TIME
—

PRUNING	
2	Late winter

PODOCARPUS

Conifer

P. andinus

P. salignus
Podocarpus

Most of the conifers in this book are to be found at your local garden centre, but Podocarpus is a rarity. It is slow-growing with oval fleshy fruits in autumn.

VARIETIES   Ⓔ

P. nivalis – 1.5 m. 1 cm long bronzy-green narrow leaves. Dwarf spreading bush. Red fruits.
P. andinus – 6 m. Bluish-green yew-like leaves. Conical tree. Pale green fruits.
P. salignus – 6 m. 10 cm long grey-green strap-like leaves. Reddish-purple fruits.

SITE & SOIL
2

PROPAGATION
1

FRUITING TIME
October

PRUNING
1

POLYGONUM

Climber

P. baldschuanicum

P. baldschuanicum
Russian Vine

The fastest way to hide an unsightly wall, ugly fence or dead tree. Masses of flowers cover the heart-shaped leaves all summer long. May need hard pruning every year.

VARIETIES   Ⓓ

P. baldschuanicum (Fallopia baldschuanica) – 15 m if left unpruned, can grow 5 m in a year. Pink-tinged pale cream. Russian or Mile-a-minute Vine. Pale green leaves. Twining growth habit — provide adequate support.
P. aubertii – 15 m if left unpruned. White. May be listed as above.

SITE & SOIL
10

PROPAGATION
1

FLOWER TIME
July — October

PRUNING	
13	Spring

PONCIRUS

Shrub

P. trifoliata

P. trifoliata
Japanese Bitter Orange

The dome-shaped bush is a tangled mass of twisted stems bearing long stout spines. Flowers appear in late spring if the previous autumn was warm.

VARIETIES   Ⓓ

P. trifoliata (Citrus trifoliata) – 2 m. White. 5 cm wide fragrant flowers are borne along the stems. The 6 cm long leaflets appear after flowering in the axils of the 3 cm long spines. Foliage is sparse. The thick-skinned wrinkled yellow fruits are 4 cm wide — they look like miniature oranges but are inedible.

SITE & SOIL
3

PROPAGATION
5

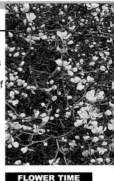

FLOWER TIME
May

PRUNING
1

POPULUS

Tree

*P. candicans
'Aurora'*

Poplar

Good specimen trees in the right situation, but not a plant for small gardens. Most are quick-growing and their roots can damage nearby drains, foundations, paths and patios.

VARIETIES Ⓓ

P. alba – 10 m. White Poplar. Leaves grey-green above, white below.
P. candicans 'Aurora' – 10 m. White- and cream-splashed young leaves. Hard prune occasionally.
P. nigra 'Italica' – 10 m. Lombardy Poplar. Tall columnar tree.
P. tremula – 4 m. Aspen. Rounded leaves constantly flutter.

SITE & SOIL
10

PROPAGATION
8

FLOWER TIME
—

PRUNING	
2	Early winter

POTENTILLA

Shrub

*P. fruticosa
'Jackman's Variety'*

*P. fruticosa
'Manchu'*

*P. fruticosa
'Tangerine'*

Shrubby Cinquefoil

There is nothing spectacular about Potentilla. The flowers, though plentiful, are not large and the foliage is not particularly eye-catching. But it is an indispensible part of millions of shrub and mixed borders because it provides floral colour while so many showier displays around it come and go. It grows in almost any type of soil in sun or light shade and requires little attention apart from annual pruning. Flowering begins in late spring and continues until early autumn. Varieties are available in many colours.

P. fruticosa 'Abbotswood'

VARIETIES Ⓓ

All the popular Potentillas are varieties of **P. fruticosa**:
P. f. 'Abbotswood' – 75 cm. White.
P. f. 'Elizabeth' – 1 m. Yellow.
P. f. 'Jackman's Variety' – 1.2 m. Yellow. Large flowers. Erect growth.
P. f. 'Katherine Dykes' – 1.5 m. Yellow.
P. f. 'Manchu' – 30 cm. White.
P. f. 'Primrose Beauty' – 1 m. Yellow. Grey-green downy leaves.
P. f. 'Princess' – 60 cm. Pink.
P. f. 'Red Ace' – 60 cm. Orange-red above, yellow below.
P. f. 'Tangerine' – 60 cm. Coppery-yellow.
P. f. 'Tilford Cream' – 60 cm. Creamy-white.

P. fruticosa 'Red Ace'

SITE & SOIL
3

PROPAGATION
1

FLOWER TIME
May — September

PRUNING	
12	Spring

PROSTANTHERA

P. cuneata
Mint Bush

Shrub

A neat bush densely covered with tiny leaves. The white-flowered species is available at many garden centres but it has not become popular. It cannot withstand heavy frost.

VARIETIES   Ⓔ

P. cuneata – 45 cm. White. 1 cm wide flowers. Leaf edges rolled — foliage emits mint-like odour when crushed. Plant against a south-facing wall. The most popular species.

P. rotundifolia – 1.5 m. Lavender. Bell-shaped flowers. More tender than P. cuneata.

P. cuneata

SITE & SOIL
2

PROPAGATION
1

FLOWER TIME
May — June

PRUNING	
13	After flowering

PRUNUS

Laurel

Shrub

The evergreen Prunus species are popular for screening and hedging. These laurels have large glossy leaves — the dense growth of the tall varieties deters intruders and hides undesirable views while the leaves of the dwarf varieties suppress weeds. Spring or early summer white flowers are followed by berries. Pruning will be necessary if the plants are to be kept in check — cut hedges in late summer. Use secateurs and not a hedge trimmer — clippings are poisonous.

P. laurocerasus

P. laurocerasus 'Otto Luyken'

VARIETIES   Ⓔ

P. laurocerasus – 4.5 m if left unpruned. White. Cherry Laurel. 12 cm high candles of small flowers in April — berries in September.

P. l. 'Rotundifolia' – Rounded leaves. Best variety for hedging.

P. l. 'Castlewellan' – 2.5 m. White-splashed grey-green leaves.

P. l. 'Otto Luyken' – 1.2 m. Compact.

P. l. 'Zabeliana' – 1.2 m. Willow-like leaves. Good floral display.

P. lusitanica – 2.5 m. White. Portugal Laurel. Differs from Cherry Laurel in several ways — leaves are smaller and red-stalked, flowers appear in early summer.

P. l. 'Variegata' – White-edged leaves.

P. laurocerasus

P. lusitanica

SITE & SOIL
4

PROPAGATION
1

P. lusitanica 'Variegata'

FLOWER TIME
Depends on species

PRUNING	
2	Late winter

PRUNUS

Shrub

P. triloba

Flowering Cherry Bush

The most spectacular varieties of flowering Prunus are the trees referred to as Flowering Cherries. There are, however, a number of shrubby forms for hedging or the border.

VARIETIES Ⓓ

Hedging types: **P. cistena** – 1.2 m. Pink. April. Red leaves. **P. cerasifera 'Nigra'** – 2 m. Pink. February-March. Purple leaves. Specimen shrub types: **P. triloba** – 2 m. Pink. Double. April. **P. tenella 'Fire Hill'** – 1.2 m. Rose-red. April. **P. incisa** – 2.5 m. White or pale pink. March.

FLOWER TIME
Depends on species

PRUNING
2   Late summer

PRUNUS

Tree

P. 'Cheal's Weeping Cherry'

Ornamental Cherry

Flowering Cherries in full bloom are one of the commonest and brightest sights in the spring garden. The usual types are 3-6 m high with white or pink flowers opening between March and May, but heights range from 1 m to 20 m and the flowering period may be as early as November or as late as June. There is a bewildering assortment to choose from and it is usual to split them up into 4 groups. The Ornamental Cherries are the largest group — the Ornamental Almonds, Peaches and Plums are detailed on the next page. Plant in early autumn.

P. hillieri 'Spire'

VARIETIES Ⓓ

Ordinary Cherries:
   P. padus – 7 m. White. Bird Cherry. Almond-scented flowers. Rounded growth.
   P. avium – 12 m. White. Wild Cherry. Attractive bark. Pyramidal growth.
   P. hillieri 'Spire' – 8 m. Pink. Vase-shaped growth.
   P. 'Pandora' – 6 m. Pink. Early. Erect growth.
   P. serrula – 6 m. White. Attractive polished bark. Arching branches.
   P. subhirtella 'Autumnalis' – White. November-March.
Japanese Cherries:
   P. 'Amanogawa' – 6 m. Pink. Columnar growth.
   P. 'Cheal's Weeping Cherry' – 6 m. Pink. Pendulous branches.
   P. 'Kanzan' – 6 m. Pink. Double. Ascending branches.
   P. 'Shirotae' – 7 m. White.
   P. 'Ukon' – 7 m. Yellow. Semi-double.

P. 'Kanzan'

FLOWER TIME
March — May

PRUNING
2   Late summer

PRUNUS

Ornamental Almond

Tree

P. dulcis

Ornamental Almonds produce their flowers in early spring before the leaves appear. The blooms are almost stalkless. They thrive in urban gardens, but do not expect ripe nuts.

VARIETIES   Ⓓ

P. dulcis (P. amygdalus) – 7 m. Pale pink. Common Almond. 2.5-5 cm wide flowers. 12 cm long finely-toothed lance-shaped leaves. Choose a sheltered spot.
P. d. 'Roseoplena' – Pink. Double.
P. amygdalo-persica 'Pollardii' – 7 m. Pink. An almond-peach hybrid — watch for peach leaf curl.

SITE & SOIL	
2	

PROPAGATION	
5	

FLOWER TIME
March

PRUNING	
2	Late summer

PRUNUS

P. davidiana

Ornamental Peach

Tree

P. persica
'Klara Mayer'

Ornamental Peaches are neither long-lived nor robust — a sheltered spot is necessary. The almost stalkless flowers appear before the leaves.

VARIETIES   Ⓓ

P. davidiana – 5 m. Pale pink. Pere David's Peach. January-February.
P. d. 'Alba' – 5 m. White.
P. persica – 4 m. Pink or red. Common Peach. April. 2.5-5 cm wide flowers. 15 cm long lance-shaped leaves.
P. p. 'Klara Mayer' – 4 m. Pink. Double.

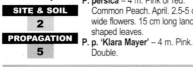

SITE & SOIL	
2	

PROPAGATION	
5	

FLOWER TIME
Depends on species

PRUNING	
2	Late summer

PRUNUS

P. spinosa

Ornamental Plum

Tree
•
Shrub

P. blireana

The flowers are produced on short stalks before or at the same time as the leaves. Foliage is sometimes purple or coppery. Some can be grown as shrubs or trees.

VARIETIES   Ⓓ

P. blireana – 5 m. Pink. Double. Coppery leaves. Purple-red fruits.
P. cerasifera – 7 m. White. Myrobalan. Red fruits.
P. c. 'Nigra' – See page 79.
P. spinosa – 3 m. White. Spiny shoots. Useful for hedging.
P. s. 'Purpurea' – 3 m. Pink. Purple leaves.

SITE & SOIL	
2	

PROPAGATION	
5	

FLOWER TIME
March — April

PRUNING	
2	Late summer

PSEUDOTSUGA

Conifer

P. menziesii

*P. menziesii
'Fletcheri'*

Douglas Fir

The Douglas Fir is too large to be grown as a specimen tree but you can use it as a tall hedge as it is not harmed by regular clipping. Not suitable for shallow or chalky soils.

VARIETIES ⓔ

P. menziesii – 4 m; 20 m or more when mature. Douglas Fir. Leaves white-banded below. Graceful lower branches bend upwards.

P. m. 'Glauca Pendula' – 2 m. Blue Douglas Fir. Bluish-green leaves. Weeping growth habit.

P. m. 'Fletcheri' – 60 cm. Bluish-green dwarf.

SITE & SOIL
9

PROPAGATION
5

FLOWER TIME
—

PRUNING
2   Early spring

PYRACANTHA

Shrub

*P. coccinea
'Lalandei'*

*P. atalantioides
'Aurea'*

Firethorn

Firethorn is a popular wall shrub, bearing masses of small flowers in late spring and then a colourful display of berries from autumn to midwinter. It can also be used as a free-standing specimen plant or an informal hedge, but remember it is a quick-growing bush and will need to be cut back regularly if planted in a confined space. It is rather similar to cotoneaster, but the leaves are toothed and the stems are spiny — wear gloves when pruning. A tough and hardy shrub, but scab and fireblight can be problems.

VARIETIES ⓔ

P. coccinea 'Lalandei' – 3.5 m. Orange-red berries.

P. c. 'Red Column' – 3.5 m. Red berries. Useful for wall cover.

P. rogersiana – 3 m. Red berries. Useful for hedging.

P. 'Mohave' – 3 m. Orange-red berries. Good fireblight resistance.

P. 'Orange Glow' – 3 m. Persistent and abundant orange berries.

P. 'Teton' – 4 m. Yellow-orange berries. Vigorous and upright.

P. 'Soleil d'Or' – 2.5 m. Yellow berries. Semi-spreading growth.

P. 'Golden Charmer' – 3 m. Yellow berries. Long arching branches.

P. atalantioides 'Aurea' – 3 m. Yellow berries. Upright growth.

SITE & SOIL
10

PROPAGATION
1

P. coccinea 'Lalandei'

P. rogersiana

BERRY TIME
October — January

PRUNING
26   After flowering

PYRUS

Tree

P. salicifolia 'Pendula'
Ornamental Pear

There are very few pear species which are grown for their ornamental leaves or flowers rather than their edible fruit. You are likely to find only one at the garden centre.

P. salicifolia 'Pendula'

SITE & SOIL
2

PROPAGATION
5

VARIETIES   Ⓓ

P. salicifolia 'Pendula' – 4 m. White. Slender, willow-like leaves covered with white wool. Small inedible fruits. Weeping growth habit. Most popular Ornamental Pear.

P. calleryana 'Chanticleer' – 6 m. White. Masses of spring flowers. Red leaves in autumn.

FLOWER TIME
April

PRUNING
2   Winter

QUERCUS

Tree

Q. cerris
Oak

A basic part of the countryside but not of the ordinary garden — nearly all are tall and spreading. There are deciduous and evergreen types in a range of leaf shapes.

Q. rubra

SITE & SOIL
23

PROPAGATION
12

VARIETIES   Ⓓ or Ⓔ

Q. robur – 8 m. English or Common Oak. Lobed oblong leaves.

Q. r. 'Fastigiata' – 6 m. Cypress Oak. Column-like growth.

Q. cerris – 10 m. Turkey Oak. Acorn cups have whiskers.

Q. ilex – 6 m. Holm Oak. Evergreen. Oval leaves.

Q. rubra – 8 m. Red autumn leaves.

FLOWER TIME
—

PRUNING
2   Winter

RHAMNUS

Shrub

R. alaternus 'Argenteovariegata'
Buckthorn

The popular variety provides a neat pyramidal shape with oval grey-green leaves which are edged in creamy-white. Some shoots may be killed if the temperature falls below -5° C.

R. alaternus 'Argenteovariegata'

SITE & SOIL
3

PROPAGATION
1

VARIETIES   Ⓓ or Ⓔ

R. alaternus 'Argenteovariegata' – 3 m. Greenish-white. Tiny flowers in spring followed by red berries in autumn. Can be trimmed to formal shapes. Provide winter protection.

R. alaternus – 3 m. All-green leaves — hardier than above.

R. frangula – 2.5 m. Small, oval green leaves. Deciduous.

BERRY TIME
September — October

PRUNING
2   Late winter

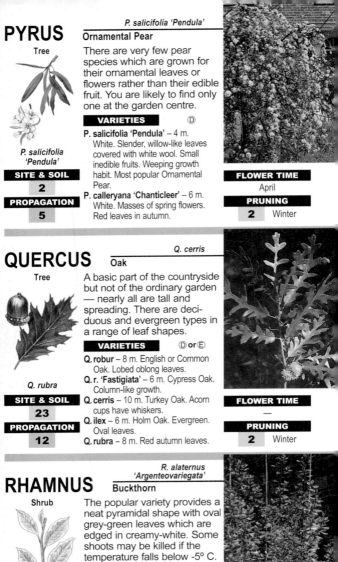

RHAPHIOLEPIS

R. umbellata
Rhaphiolepis

Shrub

A glossy-leaved shrub with a dome-shaped growth habit and a summer display of star-shaped flowers. Not fully hardy, so plant against a south-facing wall.

VARIETIES Ⓔ

R. delacourii

R. umbellata – 1.2 m. White. 1-2 cm wide flowers followed by near-black berries. Hardiest and most popular species.

SITE & SOIL
3

R. delacourii – 2 m. Pink. 10 cm wide flower clusters.

PROPAGATION
1

R. d. 'Spring Song' – Pale pink.
R. d. 'Coates' Crimson' – Red.
R. d. 'Enchantress' – Rose-pink.

FLOWER TIME
June

PRUNING	
2	Early spring

RHODODENDRON

Rhododendron

Shrub

R. 'Purple Splendour'

R. 'Elizabeth'

It is usual to regard azaleas as a separate group and they are described overleaf. The average garden rhododendron is about 1.5 m tall and blooms in May, but there are many variations — heights range from 30 cm to 6 m and the flowering time may be as early as February or as late as August. All the flower colours are there, apart from true blue, but the foliage is always evergreen and lance-shaped. Rhododendrons are shallow-rooted — mulch with peat each autumn and water copiously in dry weather.

R. 'Sappho'

VARIETIES Ⓔ

Hardy Hybrid group: Most popular varieties belong here — usual height 1.5-2.5 m, flower time April-July. Examples include **'Britannia'** (Crimson), **'Cunningham's White'** (White), **'Cynthia'** (Crimson), **'John Walter'** (Red), **'Lord Roberts'** (Dark crimson), **'Pink Pearl'** (White-edged pink), **'Purple Splendour'** (Dark purple) and **'Sappho'** (Purple-centred white).

Dwarf Hybrid group: Usual height 60-90 cm, flower time April-May. Examples include **'Elizabeth'** (Red), **'Blue Tit'** (Lavender), **'Bow Bells'** (Pink), **'Carmen'** (Crimson), **'Princess Anne'** (Yellow) and **'Snow Lady'** (White).

Species group: Numerous out-of-the-ordinary types, including **R. macabeanum** (Pale yellow), **R. arboreum** (Various) and **R. quinquefolium** (White). Most popular are **R. yakushimanum** (Pink fading to white) and its hybrids — **'Percy Wiseman'**, **'Doc'** etc.

R. yakushimanum

SITE & SOIL
24

PROPAGATION
5

FLOWER TIME
Depends on variety

PRUNING
27

RHODODENDRON — Evergreen Azalea

Shrub

R. 'Blue Danube'

R. 'Palestrina'

R. 'Vuyk's Scarlet'

R. 'Orange Beauty'

Some rhododendron varieties are traditionally referred to as 'azaleas', but there is no simple clear-cut way to distinguish an azalea from a rhododendron. Azaleas are usually daintier plants with smaller leaves, but not always. Many varieties lose their leaves in winter, but the others keep their foliage and are described here. These Evergreen or Japanese Azaleas are low growing, reaching about 60 cm-1.2 m, and in spring the spreading branches are covered in sheets of floral colour.

VARIETIES (E)

There are several types, including the large-flowered Glenn Dale and Vuyk Hybrids, the Kaempferi Hybrids and the small-flowered Kurume Hybrids.
R. 'Blue Danube' – Violet.
R. 'Addy Wery' – Orange-red. Taller than average.
R. 'Vuyk's Rosyred' – Red-throated rose. Late flowering.
R. 'Vuyk's Scarlet' – Red.
R. 'Palestrina' – White.
R. 'Mother's Day' – Red. Semi-double. Low-growing. Popular.
R. 'Orange Beauty' – Orange.
R. 'Hinomayo' – Pink. Spreading fan-like branches.
R. 'Rosebud' – Pale pink.
R. 'Blaauw's Pink' – Pink.

SITE & SOIL
24

PROPAGATION
5

R. 'Rosebud'

FLOWER TIME
April — May

PRUNING	
2	After flowering

RHODODENDRON — Deciduous Azalea

R. 'Glowing Embers'

Shrub

R. 'Cecile'

Average height 1.5-2.5 m — taller and later-flowering than Evergreen Azaleas. Rich leaf colours in autumn. Types include the Ghent, Knap Hill, Exbury and Mollis Hybrids.

VARIETIES (D)

R. 'Cecile' – Yellow-tinged pink.
R. 'Glowing Embers' – Orange.
R. 'Berryrose' – Orange-pink. Young leaves bronzy-green.
R. 'Klondyke' – Red-tinted orange. Young leaves coppery-red.
R. 'Persil' – Yellow-flushed white.
R. 'Homebush' – Dark pink. Semi-double.

SITE & SOIL
24

PROPAGATION
5

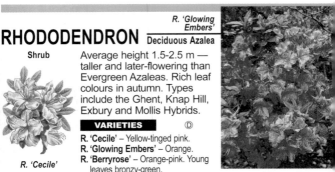

FLOWER TIME
May — June

PRUNING	
2	After flowering

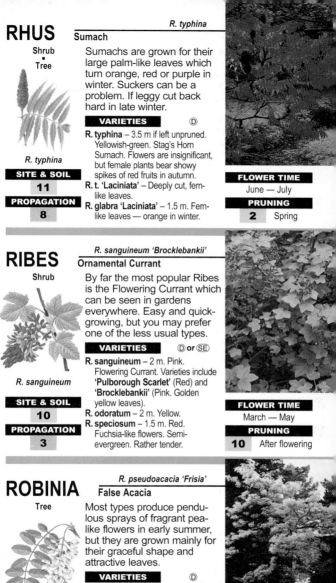

RHUS

Sumach

R. typhina

Shrub
•
Tree

Sumachs are grown for their large palm-like leaves which turn orange, red or purple in winter. Suckers can be a problem. If leggy cut back hard in late winter.

VARIETIES Ⓓ

R. typhina – 3.5 m if left unpruned. Yellowish-green. Stag's Horn Sumach. Flowers are insignificant, but female plants bear showy spikes of red fruits in autumn.

R. t. 'Laciniata' – Deeply cut, fern-like leaves.

R. glabra 'Laciniata' – 1.5 m. Fern-like leaves — orange in winter.

R. typhina

SITE & SOIL
11

PROPAGATION
8

FLOWER TIME
June — July

PRUNING
2   Spring

RIBES

Ornamental Currant

R. sanguineum 'Brocklebankii'

Shrub

By far the most popular Ribes is the Flowering Currant which can be seen in gardens everywhere. Easy and quick-growing, but you may prefer one of the less usual types.

VARIETIES Ⓓ or ⓈⒺ

R. sanguineum – 2 m. Pink. Flowering Currant. Varieties include **'Pulborough Scarlet'** (Red) and **'Brocklebankii'** (Pink. Golden yellow leaves).

R. odoratum – 2 m. Yellow.

R. speciosum – 1.5 m. Red. Fuchsia-like flowers. Semi-evergreen. Rather tender.

R. sanguineum

SITE & SOIL
10

PROPAGATION
3

FLOWER TIME
March — May

PRUNING
10   After flowering

ROBINIA

False Acacia

R. pseudoacacia 'Frisia'

Tree

Most types produce pendulous sprays of fragrant pea-like flowers in early summer, but they are grown mainly for their graceful shape and attractive leaves.

VARIETIES Ⓓ

R. pseudoacacia – 10 m; 20 m when mature. White. Leaves made up of oval leaflets — yellow in autumn. Trunk deeply furrowed. Spiny branches are brittle.

R. p. 'Frisia' – 6 m. Spreading layers of yellow foliage — coppery in autumn. Red thorns on branches.

R. p. 'Inermis' – Spineless branches.

R. pseudoacacia

SITE & SOIL
10

PROPAGATION
8

FLOWER TIME
June

PRUNING
2   Summer

ROMNEYA

R. coulteri

Tree Poppy

Shrub

There are fragrant poppies in summer and deeply-cut grey-green leaves, but this attractive plant has its problems. It is slow to establish, invasive and frost-sensitive.

VARIETIES Ⓓ

R. coulteri – 1.5 m. White. 12 cm wide flowers are borne singly at the tips of upright stems — each bloom has a central boss of golden stamens. Thicket-forming in good conditions. May not survive in cold areas.

R. coulteri

SITE & SOIL
20

PROPAGATION
8

R. 'White Cloud' (R. hybrida) – Blooms larger than above.

FLOWER TIME
July — October

PRUNING
11   March

ROSMARINUS

R. officinalis 'Miss Jessop's Upright'

Rosemary

Shrub

A good plant to grow even if you do not use its leaves in the kitchen. The upright stems are densely covered with leaves and small flowers clothe the stems in spring.

VARIETIES Ⓔ

R. officinalis – 1.5 m. Lavender. Grey-green strap-like leaves.
R. o. 'Miss Jessop's Upright' – 1.8 m. Lavender. Stiff stems.
R. o. 'Albus' – 1.5 m. White.
R. o. 'Roseus' – 1.5 m. Pink.
R. o. 'Benenden Blue' – 1.2 m. Blue. Dark green leaves. Arching stems.
R. o. 'Prostratus' – 15 cm. Blue.

R. officinalis

SITE & SOIL
2

PROPAGATION
1

FLOWER TIME
April — May

PRUNING
13   After flowering

RUBUS

R. tricolor

Evergreen Ornamental Bramble

Shrub
•
Climber

These shrubs with bristly stems are ground-covering plants with spreading shoots or tall climbers. The flowers of most varieties look like single roses.

VARIETIES ⓢⒺ or Ⓔ

R. tricolor – 3.5 m. White. Creeping plant about 30 cm high with scrambling red-bristled shoots.
R. 'Betty Ashburner' – White. Ground cover.
R. henryi 'Bambusarum' – 6 m. Pink. Glossy black fruit. Climber.
R. ulmifolius 'Bellidiflorus' – 2 m. Pink. Double. Semi-evergreen.

R. ulmifolius 'Bellidiflorus'

SITE & SOIL
10

PROPAGATION
1

FLOWER TIME
June — August

PRUNING
3   Autumn

RUBUS

Shrub

R. tridel 'Benenden'

R. cockburnianus
Deciduous Ornamental Bramble

The popular Ornamental Brambles lose their leaves in winter and are grown for their colourful stems or their flower/fruit display. Nearly all are tall with arching stems.

VARIETIES ⓓ

R. cockburnianus – 3 m. Purple. August. Whitewashed Bramble. Stems covered with white bloom.
R. thibetanus – 2 m. Whitewashed stems. Fern-like leaves.
R. tridel 'Benenden' – 3 m. White. May. 5 cm wide fragrant flowers. Arching thornless stems.
R. spectabilis – 1.5 m. Pink. April.

SITE & SOIL
10
PROPAGATION
1

FLOWER TIME
Depends on species
PRUNING
28

RUTA

Shrub

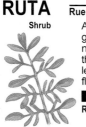

R. graveolens

R. graveolens 'Jackman's Blue'
Rue

A rounded bush once widely grown as a medicinal herb but no longer. It is now grown in the border for its decorative leaves rather than its plain flowers.

VARIETIES ⓔ

R. graveolens – 75 cm. Greenish-yellow. Blue-green leaves are deeply divided to give a filigree effect. Wear gloves when handling — the sap can cause a severe rash.
R. g. 'Jackman's Blue' – Steely blue leaves.
R. g. 'Variegata' – Cream-blotched leaves.

SITE & SOIL
4
PROPAGATION
1

FLOWER TIME
May — June
PRUNING
9   Spring

SALIX

Tree

S. chrysocoma

S. caprea 'Pendula'
Willow

Willows are attractive, but you must be careful to choose the right one. Weeping Willows need a lot of space — pick a low-growing type instead if space is limited.

VARIETIES ⓓ

S. chrysocoma – 10 m; 20 m when mature. Golden Weeping Willow. Wide-spreading. Golden shoots.
S. purpurea 'Pendula' – 5 m. Purplish shoots.
S. caprea 'Pendula' – 3 m. Kilmarnock Willow.
S. matsudana 'Tortuosa' – 10 m. Twisted stems. Non-weeping.

SITE & SOIL
23
PROPAGATION
3

FLOWER TIME
February — March
PRUNING
2   Winter

SALIX

Shrub

S. alba 'Vitellina'

Shrubby Willow

Not all willows are trees — there are low-growing shrubby varieties for the rockery as well as bold coloured-bark types for the larger garden. Damp ground is not essential.

VARIETIES   Ⓓ

S. alba varieties are grown for their coloured stems. Look for **'Vitellina'** (2 m. Yellow branches) and **'Vitellina Britzensis'** (2 m. Red).

S. lanata

S. lanata – 1 m. Yellowish-green. Erect woolly catkins. Woolly Willow. Silvery-green leaves.

SITE & SOIL
10

S. hastata 'Wehrhahnii' – 1 m. Silvery-white. Icicle-like catkins.

PROPAGATION
3

FLOWER TIME
March — April

PRUNING
28

SALVIA

Shrub

S. officinalis 'Tricolor'

Sage

Evergreen types are grown in the herb garden and border. Small flowers are produced but the decorative feature is the soft downy foliage which is available in a range of colours.

VARIETIES   Ⓔ

S. officinalis – 60 cm. Spread 1 m. Lavender. Spikes of small flowers. Grey-green leaves — a coloured-leaf variety is usually grown.

S. officinalis 'Icterina'

S. o. 'Purpurascens' – Purple.

SITE & SOIL
3

S. o. 'Icterina' – Yellow-edged green.

S. o. 'Kew Gold' – Yellow.

PROPAGATION
1

S. o. 'Tricolor' – White/pink/cream/green.

FLOWER TIME
June — July

PRUNING
11   April

SAMBUCUS

Shrub
•
Tree

S. nigra 'Marginata'

Elder

The Common Elder is a familiar sight in the country-side but there are more colour-ful types for the garden. The flowers are followed by black or red berries.

VARIETIES   Ⓓ

S. nigra – 5 m. White. Varieties include **'Aurea'** (Yellow leaves), **'Guincho Purple'** (Rose flowers. Purple leaves) and **'Marginata'** (Cream-edged leaves).

S. racemosa 'Plumosa Aurea'

S. racemosa 'Plumosa Aurea' – 2 m. Cream. Yellow leaves.

SITE & SOIL
10

S. r. 'Sunderland Gold' – Sun scorch resistant.

PROPAGATION
3

FLOWER TIME
May — June

PRUNING
8   Spring

SANTOLINA

Shrub

S. rosmarinifolia

S. chamaecyparissus
Cotton Lavender

A low-growing, mound-forming bush for use at the front of the shrub border or as low hedging. Colour comes from the silvery-grey leaves and the yellow, button-like flowers.

VARIETIES   Ⓔ

S. chamaecyparissus – 60 cm. Yellow. Flower buds sometimes removed to improve foliage display. Cut back every 2-3 years.

S. c. 'Nana' – 30 cm. Use for edging.

S. pinnata 'Edward Bowles' – 80 cm. Cream.

S. rosmarinifolia – 45 cm. Yellow. Green leaves.

SITE & SOIL
1

PROPAGATION
1

FLOWER TIME
June — August

PRUNING	
13	After flowering

SARCOCOCCA

Shrub

S. hookeriana 'Digyna'

S. hookeriana 'Humilis'
Christmas Box

Much loved by flower arrangers. The branches are used for late winter displays when they bear white or cream-coloured male and tiny female flowers.

VARIETIES   Ⓔ

S. confusa – 75 cm. Cream. Oval leaves. Black berries.

S. hookeriana 'Digyna' – 1.5 m. White. Narrow, purple-tinged leaves. Spreads by suckers.

S. h. 'Humilis' – 30 cm. White. Useful ground cover.

S. ruscifolia – 1 m. White. Dark green broad leaves. Red berries.

SITE & SOIL
10

PROPAGATION
1/8

FLOWER TIME
January — February

PRUNING	
2	After flowering

SCIADOPITYS

Conifer

S. verticillata

S. verticillata
Japanese Umbrella Pine

There is just one species and the leaf form is quite different from other conifers. The leaves look like pine needles but are arranged in whorls of 10-30 around the stems.

VARIETIES   Ⓔ

S. verticillata – 1 m; 6 m when mature. 12 cm long leaves. Peeling red bark. 10 cm cones green at first, then brown. Stake the main shoot for the first few years. Slow-growing — conical when mature. Hard to find and not easy to grow — it needs deep acid soil and some shelter from cold winds.

SITE & SOIL
24

PROPAGATION
5

FLOWER TIME
—

PRUNING
1

SENECIO

S. 'Sunshine'

Shrubby Ragwort

Shrub
•
Climber

This low and spreading shrub is often grown for its foliage rather than its flowers. The leathery oval leaves are covered with silvery hairs. Not all types are hardy.

VARIETIES Ⓔ

S. 'Sunshine' – 1 m. Yellow. May be listed as **S. greyi**, **S. laxifolius** or **Brachyglottis 'Dunedin Hybrids-Sunshine'**.

S. 'Sunshine'

SITE & SOIL
1

PROPAGATION
1

S. monroi (Brachyglottis monroi) – 1 m. Yellow. Crinkled-edged grey leaves.

S. scandens – 3 m. White. Rather tender climber.

FLOWER TIME
June — July

PRUNING
9   Spring

SEQUOIA

S. sempervirens 'Adpressa'

Californian Redwood

Conifer

The world's tallest tree is unsuitable for the garden, but it does have a couple of dwarf varieties. These are slow growing at first but may revert if not pruned each year.

VARIETIES Ⓔ

S. sempervirens – 6 m. Strap-like pointed leaves are about 1 cm long — pale green bands below. Small globular cones are borne at branch ends.

S. sempervirens

SITE & SOIL
3

PROPAGATION
5

S. s. 'Adpressa' (S. s. 'Albospica') – 1.2 m. Growing tips creamy-white.

S. 'Prostrata' – 80 cm; 1.5 m when mature. Dark green leaves.

FLOWER TIME
—

PRUNING
13   Winter

SEQUOIADENDRON

S. giganteum 'Pendulum'

Wellingtonia

Conifer

A stately giant which was widely planted in grand gardens in the 19th century. A tree to admire but not to plant in the garden. A slow-growing variety is available.

VARIETIES Ⓔ

S. giganteum – 6 m; up to 40 m when mature. Leaves are small, blue-green and awl-shaped. Branches sweep downwards to give the tree a narrow columnar shape. Oval cones hang downwards.

S. giganteum

SITE & SOIL
3

PROPAGATION
5

S. g. 'Pendulum' – 3 m. Columnar growth habit with pendent side branches. Not easy to find.

FLOWER TIME
—

PRUNING
13   Winter

SKIMMIA

Shrub

S. japonica 'Veitchii'

S. japonica 'Rubella'
Skimmia

A good choice for the front of the border. There are shiny leaves all year round and in spring there are clusters of tiny flowers followed by berries on female plants.

VARIETIES (E)

S. japonica – 1 m. White.
S. j. 'Rubella' (Male) – Pink. Red flower buds in winter.
S. j. 'Fragrans' (Male) – White. Fragrant.
S. j. 'Veitchii' (Female) – Red berries.
S. reevesiana 'Robert Fortune' (Male/female) – Pollinator partner not needed.

SITE & SOIL	PROPAGATION
18	1

FLOWER TIME
March — April

PRUNING
2   Spring

SOLANUM

Climber
•
Shrub

S. crispum 'Glasnevin'

S. jasminoides 'Album'
Perennial Nightshade

Vigorous and quick-growing but not fully hardy. There are two species — you should not have a problem with S. crispum if grown against a south- or west-facing wall.

VARIETIES (SE)

S. crispum 'Glasnevin' – 5 m. Yellow-centred mauve. 3 cm wide flowers are borne in loose clusters. Weak-stemmed shrub rather than a true climber — tying-in may be necessary.
S. jasminoides 'Album' – 6 m. White. True climber with twining stems. Needs a mild location.

SITE & SOIL	PROPAGATION
12	6

FLOWER TIME
June — October

PRUNING
3   April

SOPHORA

Shrub
•
Tree

S. tetraptera

S. microphylla
Sophora

The usual species are shrubs with yellow tubular flowers in spring but you may also find the tree-like Sophora which bears white pea-like flowers in late summer.

VARIETIES (D) or (E)

S. tetraptera – 4 m. Yellow. May. 5 cm long flowers followed by winged pods. Evergreen. Protect from frost.
S. microphylla – 3.5 m. Yellow. Hardier than S. tetraptera — leaves and flowers are smaller.
S. japonica – 7 m. White. August-September. Deciduous.

SITE & SOIL	PROPAGATION
20	1

FLOWER TIME
Depends on species

PRUNING
2   Early spring

SORBARIA

Shrub

S. aitchisonii

Tree Spiraea

A tall-stemmed shrub with long leaves which are generally silvery below. The tiny flowers are clustered on large conical heads on top of the shoots. Suckers freely.

S. arborea

VARIETIES	Ⓓ

S. aitchisonii – 3 m. Creamy-white. 30 cm high floral spikes. Leaflets sharply serrated.
S. arborea (S. kirilowii) – 4 m. White. 30 cm high floral spikes. Leaflets downy below.
S. sorbifolia – 2 m. White. 15 cm high floral spikes. Useful for the smaller garden, but invasive.

SITE & SOIL
2

PROPAGATION
1/8

FLOWER TIME
July — August

PRUNING	
8	Early spring

SORBUS

Tree

S. vilmorinii

Mountain Ash

The Sorbus you are more likely to find in the garden is the mountain ash rather than the whitebeam. It is a graceful tree with leaves made up of numerous leaflets.

S. aucuparia

VARIETIES	Ⓓ

S. aucuparia – 6 m. White. Rowan. Gold or red leaves in autumn.
S. a. 'Asplenifolia' – 6 m. Fern-like leaves.
S. a. 'Fastigiata' – 5 m. Columnar.
S. cashmiriana – 6 m. Pale pink. White berries. Fern-like leaves.
S. vilmorinii – 6 m. White. White or pink berries. Feathery leaves.

SITE & SOIL
10

PROPAGATION
5

FLOWER TIME
May — June

PRUNING	
2	Winter

SORBUS

Tree

S. aria 'Lutescens'

Whitebeam

The whitebeams have oval leaves which are green above and grey or white below, turning yellow in autumn. The late spring flowers are followed by oval berries in autumn.

S. intermedia

VARIETIES	Ⓓ

S. aria 'Lutescens' – 7 m; 12 m when mature. White. Young leaves are silvery-white — later green above and grey below.
S. intermedia – 6 m; 10 m when mature. White. Swedish White-beam. Leaves yellow-grey below.
S. thibetica 'John Mitchell' – 5 m. White. Large leaves, white below.

SITE & SOIL
10

PROPAGATION
5

FLOWER TIME
May — June

PRUNING	
2	Winter

SPARTIUM

Spanish Broom

Shrub

S. junceum

The green rush-like stems are clothed with yellow pea-like flowers throughout the summer. Foliage is sparse. It soon becomes gaunt in the wrong situation.

VARIETIES   Ⓓ

S. junceum – 3 m if left unpruned. Yellow. 3 cm long fragrant flowers. Green stems provide an evergreen effect in winter. Usually grown as a loose bush but can be trained as a standard. Annual pruning is necessary if site is not sandy and unshaded. Only one species is available.

SITE & SOIL
20

PROPAGATION
1

FLOWER TIME
June — September

PRUNING
9   March

SPIRAEA

Spiraea

Shrub

S. arguta

S. vanhouttei

S. japonica
'Anthony Waterer'

SITE & SOIL
10

PROPAGATION
1/3

Spiraeas are popular and have a well-deserved reputation for being easy to grow and free-flowering. The only drawbacks are the need for annual pruning and the thicket-forming habit of some of the larger suckering species. The spring-flowering group bear tiny white flowers in clusters on arching stems. The summer-flowering types are shorter and more compact with white, pink or red flowers in flat heads, round domes or upright spikes — the low-growing varieties can be cut back hard in early spring.

VARIETIES   Ⓓ

Spring-flowering group:
S. arguta – 2 m. White. April-May. Blooms festoon arching stems.
S. nipponica 'Snowmound' – 1 m. Green-centred white. June.
S. thunbergii – 1 m. White. March-April. Yellow leaves in autumn.
S. vanhouttei – 2.5 m. White. May. Thicket-forming.
Summer-flowering group:
S. japonica 'Anthony Waterer' – 1 m. Pink. July-September.
S. j. 'Goldflame' – 1 m. Crimson. July-August. Young leaves golden.
S. j. 'Shirobana' – 1.2 m. White and pink flower-heads on the same plant. July-September.

S. nipponica 'Snowmound'

S. japonica 'Goldflame'

FLOWER TIME
Depends on species

PRUNING
8   After flowering

93

STACHYURUS

S. praecox
Stachyurus

Shrub

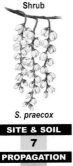

S. praecox

A late winter-flowering alternative to winter jasmine and witch hazel. Cup-shaped blooms are borne on pendent flower-heads. A hardy plant — use for indoor decoration.

VARIETIES	Ⓓ

S. praecox – 2.5 m. Pale yellow. 5-8 cm long catkin-like flower-heads bear about 20 blooms. Flowers appear before oval leaves open.

SITE & SOIL
7

PROPAGATION
1

S. chinensis – 2.5 m. Similar to above, but flower-heads are longer with more blooms.

S. 'Magpie' – 2.5 m. Cream-edged leaves.

FLOWER TIME
February — March

PRUNING
8   After flowering

STEPHANANDRA

S. incisa
'Crispa'
Stephanandra

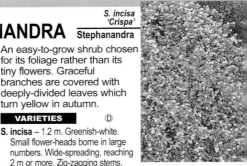

Shrub

S. incisa
'Crispa'

An easy-to-grow shrub chosen for its foliage rather than its tiny flowers. Graceful branches are covered with deeply-divided leaves which turn yellow in autumn.

VARIETIES	Ⓓ

S. incisa – 1.2 m. Greenish-white. Small flower-heads borne in large numbers. Wide-spreading, reaching 2 m or more. Zig-zagging stems.

SITE & SOIL
15

PROPAGATION
1/10

S. i. 'Crispa' – 60 cm. Creamy-white. Leaves small and deeply cut.

S. tanakae – 2 m. White. Maple-like leaves turn gold in autumn. Grown for its reddish stems.

FLOWER TIME
June — July

PRUNING
8   Late summer

STEWARTIA

S. malacodendron
Stewartia

Shrub
•
Tree

S. ovata

A bush or tree with large white flowers — a plant for the woodland garden in the southern counties. You will have to look through the catalogues to find one.

VARIETIES	Ⓓ

S. malacodendron – 5 m. White. 8 cm wide flowers have showy purple anthers. Bushy growth.

SITE & SOIL
14

PROPAGATION
5

S. ovata – 5 m. White. 10 cm wide flowers have showy orange stamens. Bushy growth.

S. pseudocamellia – 5 m; 12 m when mature. White. Columnar tree. Attractive peeling bark.

FLOWER TIME
June — July

PRUNING
2   Winter

STRANVAESIA

S. davidiana
'Fructuluteo'
Stranvaesia

Shrub

S. davidiana

A spreading shrub with lance-shaped leaves. Hawthorn-like flower-heads appear in early summer and these are followed by bunches of bright berries.

VARIETIES Ⓔ

S. davidiana – 3 m. White. Red berries persist all winter. Narrow leathery leaves turn red in winter.
S. d. 'Palette' – 2 m. White. Cream-edged green leaves. Slow growing.
S. d. 'Fructuluteo' – 2 m. Yellow berries.
S. d. 'Prostrata' – 30 cm. Ground cover plant.

SITE & SOIL
4

PROPAGATION
1/6

BERRY TIME
September — January

PRUNING
2   Spring

STYRAX

S. japonica
Snowbell

Shrub
•
Tree

S. obassia

Not often seen — the most popular species (S. japonica) needs both ample space and some protection from the morning sun. The flowers look like open-mouthed snowdrops.

VARIETIES Ⓓ

S. japonica – 3 m; 6 m when mature. White. Japanese Snowbell. 3 cm wide flowers borne in clusters along branches. Horizontal branches droop at the tips.
S. j. 'Pink Chimes' – 3 m. Pink.
S. obassia – 3 m. White. Long pendent flower-heads. Round leaves. Narrow growth habit.

SITE & SOIL
7

PROPAGATION
5

FLOWER TIME
June

PRUNING
2   Spring

SYMPHORICARPOS

S. doorenbosii
'Mother of Pearl'
Snowberry

Shrub

S. albus

A grow-anywhere plant — in full sun or dense shade, in rich or poor soil. Use it to cover large areas of the wilder part of the garden. Berries remain for months.

VARIETIES Ⓓ

S. albus – 2 m. Pink. White berries. Suckers freely.
S. laevigatus – 2 m. Pink. Abundant white berries. Blue stems.
S. orbiculatus 'Variegatus' – 1 m. Yellow-edged leaves — needs sun.
S. doorenbosii 'Mother of Pearl' – 1.2 m. Pink-flushed white berries. Drooping stems. Does not sucker.

SITE & SOIL
16

PROPAGATION
3/8

BERRY TIME
October — January

PRUNING
8   Early spring

SYRINGA

Lilac

Shrub

The types which brighten up gardens in late May are nearly always varieties of S. vulgaris, the Common Lilac. The flowers are borne in conical spires — colours range from white to dark purple and heights can exceed 4 m. The popular varieties will grow in all sorts of soil, but do not neglect them. Feed and mulch every year and both suckers and dead blooms should be removed. The flowering season is short (about three weeks), but the fragrance and the size of the blooms compensate for it.

S. vulgaris 'Maud Notcutt'

S. vulgaris 'Souvenir de Louis Spaeth'

S. vulgaris 'Madame Lemoine'

VARIETIES   Ⓓ

S. vulgaris – 1.5-3 m. Various. Single-flowered varieties include **'Primrose'** (Pale yellow), **'Sensation'** (White-edged red), **'Firmament'** (Lilac), **'Souvenir de Louis Spaeth'** (Red) and **'Maud Notcutt'** (White). Double-flowered varieties include **'Charles Joly'** (Dark red), **'Katherine Havemeyer'** (Lavender) and **'Madame Lemoine'** (White).

S. microphylla 'Superba'

S. microphylla 'Superba' – 1.5 m. Pink. Small leaves.

S. persica

SITE & SOIL
11

S. persica – 1 m. Mauve. Small clusters of flowers. Small leaves.

S. meyeri – 80 cm. Lilac.

S. josiflexa 'Bellicent' – 3 m. Pink. Large plume-like flower-heads.

PROPAGATION
5

FLOWER TIME
May — June

PRUNING	
2	After flowering

TAMARIX

Tamarisk

T. tetrandra

Shrub

The tiny leaves and the tall plumes of small flowers combine to give a unique feathery effect. It will become a tall gaunt bush if not pruned annually.

VARIETIES   Ⓓ

T. tetrandra – 2.5 m. Pink. May-June. 60 cm high plumes of flowers at the top of branches before scale-like leaves appear. Prune when blooms fade.

T. ramosissima

SITE & SOIL
2

T. ramosissima (T. pentandra) – 2.5 m. Pink. August-September. Fragrant flowers. Prune in February.

T. r. 'Rubra' – 2.5 m. Dark pink.

PROPAGATION
3

FLOWER TIME
Depends on species

PRUNING	
12	Depends on species

TAXODIUM

Conifer

T. distichum
Swamp Cypress

A graceful tree, conical when young and rounded when mature. Thrives in wet ground but it will grow in any chalk-free loamy soil. Feathery foliage falls in autumn.

T. distichum

VARIETIES	Ⓓ

T. distichum – 5 m; up to 30 m when mature. Leaves turn bronzy-yellow in autumn. Rounded 3 cm wide cones. Reddish fibrous bark. Mature specimens produce above-ground growths ('cypress knees') from the roots in wet conditions.

T. d. 'Imbricatum' – Narrow cone shape.

SITE & SOIL
13

PROPAGATION
5

FLOWER TIME
—

PRUNING
1

TAXUS

Conifer

Yew

A slow-growing conifer which is widely used for hedging, but there are other shapes ranging from prostrate ground covers to tall column-like trees. Dark green is the usual colour, but there are several golden varieties. Yew is more tolerant of unfavourable conditions than most other conifers, but it cannot tolerate badly-drained soil which is waterlogged in winter. Male and female flowers are borne on separate plants — the females bear 1.5 cm wide fleshy red fruits which contain a single seed. Leaves and fruits are poisonous.

T. baccata 'Fastigiata'

T. baccata

VARIETIES	Ⓔ

T. baccata – 2 m; 12 m when mature. English Yew. Large shrub or upright small tree usually grown as a hedge. 2-4 cm long leaves borne in two rows. For a specimen tree choose a variety.

T. b. 'Fastigiata' – 1.5 m; 5 m when mature. Irish Yew. Narrow column when young, spreading a little with age. Blackish-green leaves.

T. b. 'Fastigiata Aureomarginata' – 1.5 m; 5 m when mature. Golden Irish Yew. Yellow-edged leaves — the tree is dull gold in winter. Male.

T. b. 'Fastigiata Aurea' – Yellow-splashed leaves.

T. b. 'Standishii' – Dwarf variety of Irish Yew.

T. b. 'Semperaurea' – 60 cm. Bright yellow leaves in spring. Male.

T. b. 'Repandens' – 60 cm. Ground cover spreading to 3 m or more.

T. media 'Hicksii' – 1.5 m. Dark green columnar bush.

T. baccata 'Semperaurea'

SITE & SOIL
4

PROPAGATION
5

FLOWER TIME
—

PRUNING	
2	Spring

TEUCRIUM

Germander

Shrub

T. chamaedrys

Stems bear heads of two-lipped flowers. The two most popular species differ in size, flower colour, cultural needs, hardiness and flower-head shape.

VARIETIES   Ⓔ

T. fruticans – 1.5 m. Pale blue. Shrubby Germander. Small orchid-like flowers borne in whorls at stem tips. Silvery-grey stems. Needs wall protection.

T. f. 'Compactum' – 80 cm dwarf.

T. chamaedrys – 30 cm. Pink. Wall Germander. Flowers borne on spikes. Hardy.

SITE & SOIL
1

PROPAGATION
1

FLOWER TIME
July — September

PRUNING
2   Spring

THUJA

Arbor-vitae

Conifer

T. occidentalis

There is a range of shapes and sizes — dwarfs for the rockery, specimen trees for the lawn and vigorous varieties for hedging. It is easy to mistake Thuja for the much more popular Chamaecyparis — both have flattened sprays of tiny, scale-like leaves. To tell the difference crush a branchlet — nearly all Thujas are aromatic. The cones are the key difference — Thuja cones are elongated with outward-turning scales. Thujas are generally not difficult to grow, but badly-drained soil can be fatal.

T. occidentalis 'Hetz Midg

VARIETIES   Ⓔ

T. occidentalis – There are many varieties:

T. o. 'Rheingold' – 1 m. Conical or rounded. Gold in summer, coppery in winter.

T. o. 'Golden Globe' – 60 cm. Spherical. Year-round golden leaves.

T. o. 'Danica' – 40 cm. Spherical. Dark green in summer, bronze in winter.

T. o. 'Holmstrup' – 2 m. Narrowly conical. Green.

T. o. 'Smaragd' – 2.5 m. Pyramid-shaped — a good hedging variety. Green.

T. o. 'Hetz Midget' – 20 cm. Spherical. One of the smallest of all conifers. Dark green.

T. orientalis 'Aurea Nana' – 60 cm. Oval. Yellow in summer, bronze in winter.

T. plicata – 5 m. Green.

T. p. 'Zebrina' – 4 m. Yellow-banded leaves.

T. orientalis 'Aurea Nana

SITE & SOIL
3

PROPAGATION
5

FLOWER TIME
—

PRUNING
24

TILIA

Lime

T. 'Petiolaris'

Tree

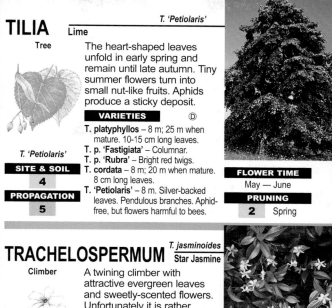

The heart-shaped leaves unfold in early spring and remain until late autumn. Tiny summer flowers turn into small nut-like fruits. Aphids produce a sticky deposit.

VARIETIES   Ⓓ

T. platyphyllos – 8 m; 25 m when mature. 10-15 cm long leaves.
T. p. 'Fastigiata' – Columnar.
T. p. 'Rubra' – Bright red twigs.
T. cordata – 8 m; 20 m when mature. 8 cm long leaves.
T. 'Petiolaris' – 8 m. Silver-backed leaves. Pendulous branches. Aphid-free, but flowers harmful to bees.

T. 'Petiolaris'

SITE & SOIL
4

PROPAGATION
5

FLOWER TIME
May — June

PRUNING
2   Spring

TRACHELOSPERMUM

T. jasminoides
Star Jasmine

Climber

A twining climber with attractive evergreen leaves and sweetly-scented flowers. Unfortunately it is rather tender and needs a south- or west-facing wall.

VARIETIES   Ⓔ

T. asiaticum – 6 m. Yellow-centred cream. 2 cm wide flat-faced fragrant flowers. Most reliable species.
T. jasminoides – 8 m. White, changing to cream. Confederate Jasmine. Large flowers.
T. j. 'Variegatum' – Cream-splashed leaves.
T. j. 'Wilsonii' – Red leaves in winter.

T. asiaticum

SITE & SOIL
9

PROPAGATION
1

FLOWER TIME
July — August

PRUNING
2   March

TRACHYCARPUS

T. fortunei
Windmill Palm

Tree

Only one palm (the Chusan or Chinese Windmill Palm) can be considered to be hardy. It will withstand winter frosts in most areas but it still needs protection against icy winds.

VARIETIES   Ⓔ

T. fortunei – 3 m. Yellow. Large arching heads of small flowers. Round black fruits in autumn. The much-divided fan-shaped leaves are up to 1 m wide. Leaf stalks toothed. Stout unbranched trunk bears clusters of stiff leaves on the top. The only species you are likely to find.

T. fortunei

SITE & SOIL
2

PROPAGATION
5

FLOWER TIME
June

PRUNING
16   Early spring

TSUGA

Conifer

T. canadensis

Hemlock

Thin yew-like branches arch at the tips and give the tree or shrub a graceful appearance. Small, egg-shaped cones are borne at the ends of the branchlets.

VARIETIES Ⓔ

T. canadensis – 3 m; 25 m when mature. Eastern Hemlock. Leaves white-banded below.

T. c. 'Pendula' – 60 cm. Drooping.

T. heterophylla – 3.5 m; 30 m when mature. Western Hemlock. Leaves vary in size — white below. Xmas-tree appearance. Requires moist soil.

SITE & SOIL
7

PROPAGATION
5

FLOWER TIME
—

PRUNING
1

ULEX

Shrub

U. europaeus 'Flore Pleno'

U. gallii 'Mizen Head'

Gorse

An excellent shrub for hedging or large-scale ground cover if the site is right. It needs sandy or stony soil and an absence of shade. All are spiny. Dislikes transplanting.

VARIETIES Ⓔ

U. europaeus – 2 m. Yellow. Common Gorse or Furze. Pea-like flowers in spring, and occasionally in summer and autumn. Do not dig up plants growing wild.

U. e. 'Flore Pleno' – 1.5 m. Yellow. Semi-double.

U. gallii 'Mizen Head' – 60 cm. Yellow. Autumn flowering.

SITE & SOIL
20

PROPAGATION
1

FLOWER TIME
Depends on species

PRUNING
13   After flowering

ULMUS

Tree

U. glabra

U. parvifolia 'Geisha'

Elm

Dutch Elm Disease has swept away countless trees. There is no cure — diseased branches must be cut and burnt and badly affected trees must be felled and removed.

VARIETIES Ⓓ

All species such as **U. procera**, **U. glabra** etc have oval, toothed and distinctly lop-sided leaves. Choose one noted for disease resistance:

U. parvifolia – 15 m when mature. Leaves remain until New Year.

U. p. 'Frosty' – White-toothed leaves.

U. p. 'Geisha' – Dwarf. White-edged leaves.

SITE & SOIL
3

PROPAGATION
5

FLOWER TIME
—

PRUNING
2   Autumn

VACCINIUM

V. floribundum

Vaccinium

Shrub

Acid lovers which bear urn-shaped flowers. Species vary widely — upright or spreading, deciduous or evergreen, spring- or summer-flowering, red or black berries.

VARIETIES Ⓓ or Ⓢ or Ⓔ

V. corymbosum – 1.2 m. White or pale pink. May. Black fruits. Red autumn leaves. Deciduous.

V. cylindraceum – 3 m. Semi-evergreen.

V. floribundum – 1 m. Pink. June. Red berries. Evergreen.

V. nummularia – 30 cm. Pink-edged white. June. Evergreen.

V. nummularia

SITE & SOIL
14

PROPAGATION
1

FLOWER TIME
Depends on species

PRUNING
2 Late winter

VIBURNUM

Viburnum

Shrub

This large genus has varieties to produce colour all year round and to suit almost every purpose — ground cover, screening, specimen plants and bushes for the border. A wide assortment, but they do have some features in common. All are easy to grow and will succeed in chalky soil. There is no need for regular pruning and all are hardy. They are divided into three basic groups in the list below and are deciduous unless indicated. Each group contains one or more garden favourites.

V. bodnantense

V. tinus 'Gwenllian'

V. opulus 'Sterile'

VARIETIES Ⓓ or Ⓔ

Winter-flowering group: Prefer full sun.
V. tinus – 3 m. White, pink buds. December-April. Large oval leaves. Evergreen. Popular varieties include **'Eve Price'** and **'Gwenllian'**.
V. farreri – 2.5 m. White. November-February.
V. bodnantense – 2.5 m. Pink. January-March.
Spring-flowering group: Prefer light shade.
V. opulus 'Sterile' – 2.5 m. White. May-June. Ball-like flower-heads.
V. plicatum – 1.8 m. White. May-June. Flat flower-heads. Tiered branches.
V. burkwoodii – 2 m. White. April-May. Evergreen.
Autumn-berrying group: Bright autumn leaves.
V. davidii – 60 cm. White. June. Blue berries. Evergreen.
V. opulus – 3 m. White. June. Red berries.

V. farreri

SITE & SOIL
7

PROPAGATION
1

FLOWER TIME
Depends on species

PRUNING
2 May

VINCA

Shrub

V. minor

V. major 'Variegata'

Periwinkle

The trailing stems of the lowly periwinkle root into the soil as they spread and the tangled mat of shoots and oval leaves provide an effective ground cover around taller shrubs.

VARIETIES Ⓔ

V. major – 25 cm high. Blue. 3 cm wide flowers. Very invasive.
V. m. 'Variegata' – Cream-edged green leaves.
V. minor – 10 cm high. Blue. Small flowers, narrow leaves. Varieties include **'Atropurpurea'** (Purple) and **'Aureovariegata'** (Blue, white-edged leaves).

SITE & SOIL
4

PROPAGATION
10/8

FLOWER TIME
March — May

PRUNING
13 Spring

VITIS

Climber

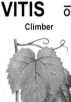

V. coignetiae

V. vinifera 'Purpurea'

Ornamental Vine

Vitis is usually grown for its fruit, but several are planted for the glowing colour of their autumn foliage. Vitis is not self-clinging so some form of support is necessary.

VARIETIES Ⓓ

V. coignetiae – 12 m. 25 cm wide leaves. Orange and red leaves in autumn. Tasteless purple grapes.
V. 'Brandt' – 9 m. Large lobed leaves. Orange and pink leaves in autumn. Sweet purple grapes.
V. vinifera 'Purpurea' – 5 m. Leaves change from red to purple in autumn. Tasteless purple grapes.

SITE & SOIL
4

PROPAGATION
1

FRUITING TIME
October

PRUNING
2 Winter

WEIGELA

Shrub

W. florida 'Variegata'

W. 'Bristol Ruby'

Weigela

Weigela does best when it is pruned annually and grown in fertile soil, but it will succeed almost anywhere and with-stands the neglect it receives in millions of gardens.

VARIETIES Ⓓ

W. florida 'Variegata' – 1.2 m. Pale pink. Variegated leaves.
W. f. 'Foliis Purpureis' – 1.2 m. Pink. Dark purple leaves.
W. 'Bristol Ruby' – 2 m. Red.
W. 'Briant Rubidor' – 1.5 m. Red. Yellow or green/yellow leaves.
W. middendorffiana – 1.2 m. Orange-marked yellow.

SITE & SOIL
10

PROPAGATION
3

FLOWER TIME
May — June

PRUNING
10 After flowering

WISTERIA

W. floribunda
'Macrobotrys'

Wistaria

Climber

W. sinensis

The twining stems covered with hanging trails of pea-like flowers are a familiar sight in late spring. Buy a container-grown specimen and plant in a sunny, sheltered spot.

VARIETIES   Ⓓ

W. sinensis – 15 m. Lilac. Chinese Wistaria. Fragrant blooms in 30 cm long flower-heads.
W. s. 'Alba' – White.
W. floribunda – 8 m. Blue. Japanese Wistaria. 20 cm long flower-heads.
W. f. 'Macrobotrys' – 8 m. Lilac. 70 cm long flower-heads.

SITE & SOIL
11

PROPAGATION
5/6

FLOWER TIME
May — June

PRUNING
17   July

YUCCA

Y. gloriosa

Yucca

Shrub

Y. filamentosa

The large sword-like leaves and immense flower-heads give an exotic touch to a border or patio tub. Quite hardy, but it takes about 3 years for flowering to start.

VARIETIES   Ⓔ

Y. filamentosa – White. 60 cm long stiff leaves with white threads along the edges. 1.5 m high flower stalks.
Y. f. 'Bright Edge' – Yellow-edged leaves.
Y. flaccida – White. Leaves less rigid than Y. filamentosa.
Y. gloriosa – Take care; leaves are bayonet-tipped.

SITE & SOIL
2

PROPAGATION
8

FLOWER TIME
July — August

PRUNING
16   Spring

ZENOBIA

Z. pulverulenta

Zenobia

Shrub

Z. pulverulenta

An unusual companion for the popular lime-haters such as Calluna, Camellia and Rhododendron. There is no good reason for its rarity — it is hardy and colourful.

VARIETIES   ⓈⒺ

Z. pulverulenta (**Z. speciosa**) – 1 m. White. Clusters of 1 cm wide pendent bell-like flowers with aniseed-like fragrance. 5 cm long oval leaves. Young stems and leaves silvery in spring, changing to green. Stems and leaves turn orange in autumn. Open arching growth habit.

SITE & SOIL
24

PROPAGATION
1

FLOWER TIME
June — July

PRUNING
10   After flowering

CHAPTER 3

BUYING

SOURCES OF SUPPLY

Nowadays the garden centre is the main source of supply. It is easy to understand why — neat rows of an extensive range of plants all laid out for you to see. But it need not be your only source — where money is short there are cheaper ways to buy the popular sorts and where rarities are wanted it may be necessary to buy from a mail order nursery.

GARDEN CENTRE

The garden centre is the only place to go if you want to choose from a large selection for immediate planting. A visit is one of the joys of gardening, but a few words of advice — go at the start of the planting season, avoid weekends if you can and do not buy on impulse. Always check the suitability of a plant before you buy.

Advantages: You can see exactly what you are buying and you can take it home with you, which means no delays and no transport charges. At larger garden centres there is help on hand, but do check the advice in the A-Z guide.

Drawbacks: The varieties on offer are usually the more popular sorts and the number of any one variety may be limited — for a massed planting or a hedge you may have to order from a nursery. Garden centres are generally out of town — you will need a car.

If something goes wrong: Take the plant back and explain what happened. You will need proof of purchase.

BARGAIN OFFER NURSERY

The 'bargain offers' advertised in newspapers and magazines are sometimes good value, but don't expect too much. However, caution is needed with the 'wonder offers' — phrases such as 'everlasting blooms', 'continuous sheets of colour' etc should not be taken too literally.

Advantages: An inexpensive way to obtain old favourites which are known for their toughness and reliability.

Drawbacks: If the plants are truly cheap, there must be a reason. The shrubs may be only rooted cuttings which will take time to establish or they may be substandard or damaged stock.

If something goes wrong: Complain if the plants are dead or diseased, but not if they are smaller than expected.

MAIL ORDER NURSERY

Mail order nurseries remain an important source of supply. Try to choose one with a good reputation, one you have used before or one which has been recommended to you. Order early in the season and fill out the form carefully.

Advantages: There is often an excellent catalogue from which you can choose your requirements in the peace and comfort of your own home. Rarities as well as popular ones can be obtained from the larger nurseries and there are establishments which specialise in particular groups such as heathers and roses.

Drawbacks: Obviously you cannot see what you are buying and you cannot take your order home with you. This means that the shrubs may arrive when planting is inconvenient. Some of the plants on your order may be out of stock and the delivery charge on container-grown and balled plants may be high.

If something goes wrong: Write to the company and explain what has happened if you are sure it was not your fault. Some nurseries will return your money.

HIGH STREET SHOP

In autumn and spring many popular varieties are sold at greengrocers, department stores, supermarkets etc — they are usually available as bare-rooted plants in labelled polythene bags.

Advantages: You can pick up a shrub while doing your everyday shopping — only a virtue if your plot is small and a trip to a garden centre is a chore. A more important advantage is that pre-packaged shrubs are cheaper than container-grown ones.

Drawbacks: The selection is limited as only fast-moving lines can be stocked, and warm conditions in store can lead to drying-out.

If something goes wrong: You can try complaining to the shop, but the response will depend on the policy of the store.

OWN-GROWN

The idea of raising your own stock from cuttings in a cold frame or propagator may seem like too much work, but there are many varieties which can be propagated from cuttings stuck in the ground in late autumn or by layering, and that involves no aftercare. Get cuttings from your own garden or from a friend — don't steal cuttings from public gardens.

Advantages: The plants are free and there is the satisfaction of having grown your own.

Drawbacks: It takes time for a stem cutting to root and so there is an inevitable delay before the new shrub is ready for planting where it is to grow.

If something goes wrong: If roots fail to develop, try to find out why — learn from your mistakes.

PLANTING MATERIAL

Poor planting rather than poor stock is the usual cause of failure, but it is still necessary to choose wisely and carefully at buying time — look for the bad signs described below. There are four basic types of planting material and each one has its own advantages and disadvantages. The choice is up to you, but if you propose to plant in summer then you must choose a container-grown specimen.

BALLED

The traditional way to buy evergreens. Suitable for planting in September, October or April.

Evergreens are occasionally still sold as balled plants. The specimen is dug up at the nursery and the soil ball is tightly wrapped in hessian sacking, nylon netting or polythene sheeting. When moving a balled plant make sure you hold it under the sacking — never use the stems as a handle. Look at the plant carefully before purchase. Feel for strong girdling roots through the sacking — they run horizontally near the top of the soil ball and are a bad sign. The soil should be firm and moist and the leaves and stems should be healthy.

PRE-PACKAGED

The popular way to buy deciduous shrubs from shops and department stores. Suitable for planting between October and March.

Pre-packaged shrubs are the standard planting material sold by hardware shops, department stores and super-markets. The pre-packaged plant is a bare-rooted specimen with its roots surrounded by moist peat and the whole plant packed into a plastic bag. Labels are descriptive and colourful, and such plants are cheaper than their container-grown counterparts, but there are drawbacks. It may be hard to see what you are buying and premature growth may occur in the warm conditions in the shop. So look for the standard bare-rooted danger signs — leaf buds beginning to open, shrivelled or diseased stems and small white roots growing into the peat.

CONTAINER-GROWN

The most convenient way to buy both deciduous and evergreen shrubs. Suitable for planting all year round.

A container-grown plant may be expensive but it has one great advantage — it can be planted at any time of the year as long as the soil is suitable and the weather is reasonable. It is not, however, a fool-proof method of planting shrubs — you have to choose and plant with care. Look for danger signs before you buy — these include wilted or diseased leaves, split container, dry soil and a thick root growing through the base. Don't buy the biggest size you can afford — large and old specimens take a long time to establish and are often overtaken by younger and less expensive ones. A rooted cutting in a plant pot is cheaper than an established specimen which is growing in a container, but you will often have to wait some time for it to reach flowering size. At planting time make sure that the earth around the soil ball is enriched with organic matter — roots hate to move from a peat compost into a mineral soil.

BARE-ROOTED

The traditional way to buy deciduous shrubs. Suitable for planting between October and March.

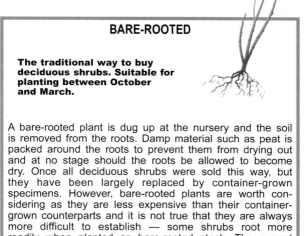

A bare-rooted plant is dug up at the nursery and the soil is removed from the roots. Damp material such as peat is packed around the roots to prevent them from drying out and at no stage should the roots be allowed to become dry. Once all deciduous shrubs were sold this way, but they have been largely replaced by container-grown specimens. However, bare-rooted plants are worth considering as they are less expensive than their container-grown counterparts and it is not true that they are always more difficult to establish — some shrubs root more readily when planted as bare-rooted stock. The correct time for planting is during the dormant season. Examine the plant carefully if you are buying from a shop, nursery or market stall. Reject it if the leaf buds are beginning to open, if the stems are shrivelled or diseased or if there are small white roots growing into the peat.

CHAPTER 4

PLANTING

TIMING

CONTAINER-GROWN

JULY	AUG	SEPT	OCT	NOV	DEC	JAN	FEB	MARCH	APRIL	MAY	JUNE

| BALLED | BARE-ROOTED & | BALLED |
| EVERGREENS | PRE-PACKAGED | EVERGREENS |

Container-grown plants can be planted at any time, but it is advisable to avoid the depths of winter and midsummer. The time for planting bare-rooted and pre-packaged plants is much more restricted. The best time is between mid October and late November, but if the weather is abnormally wet or if the soil is heavy then it is better to wait until March. Soil conditions are as important as the calendar. The ground should be neither frozen nor waterlogged. Squeeze a handful of soil — it should be wet enough to form a ball and yet dry enough to shatter when dropped on to a hard surface.

SPACING

**Recommended
Planting Distance
for most shrubs**

Add the mature height of A and the mature height of B (check A-Z guide). Divide the answer by 3 for the recommended planting distance

**PLANTING
DISTANCE**

Planting too closely is a common problem. It is easy to see why people do this — the plants are usually small, and it is hard to imagine what they will look like when they are mature. When you plant at the recommended distance the border will look bare and unattractive. One solution is to plant a number of 'fill-in' shrubs between the choice shrubs you have planted. These 'fill-in' shrubs should be inexpensive old favourites and are progressively removed as the choice shrubs develop. A second alternative is to fill the space between the planted shrubs with bulbs, bedding plants and/or herbaceous perennials.

GETTING READY FOR PLANTING

BALLED PLANT

Balled plants can be left unplanted for several weeks provided the soil ball is kept moist

Keep the soil ball moist until you are ready to plant

To prevent the plant from toppling over, secure the stem to a firm support if planting is to be delayed

Do *not* remove the covering at this stage

CONTAINER-GROWN PLANT

Container-grown plants can be left unplanted for several weeks provided the soil is kept moist

If the shrub is tall, secure the stem to a firm support if planting is to be delayed

Keep the roots moist by watering the soil until you are ready to plant

Cut off any leaves and dead flowers

Cut off decayed or abnormally thin shoots

BARE-ROOTED PLANT

Bare-rooted plants can be left unplanted for 3-4 days provided the peat is kept moist

Plunge roots in a bucket of water for about 2 hours if they appear dry or if the stems are shrivelled. Roots must never be allowed to dry out before planting. Cut back to about 30 cm

PLANTING

CONTAINER-GROWN PLANT

PLANTING MIXTURE
Make up the planting
mixture in a wheel-
barrow on a day when
the soil is reasonably
dry and friable —
1 part topsoil and
1 part moist peat.
Keep this mixture
in a shed until
you are ready
to start
planting

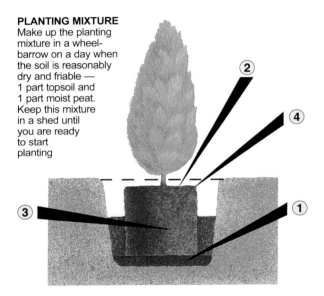

(1) The hole should be deep enough to ensure that the top of the soil ball will be about 2.5 cm below the soil surface after planting. The hole should be wide enough for the soil ball to be surrounded by a 7.5-10 cm layer of planting mixture. Put a 2.5 cm layer of planting mixture (see above) at the bottom of the hole

(2) The container should have been watered thoroughly at least an hour before planting. Remove the plant carefully from the container. Stand the root ball on a piece of plastic sheeting

(3) Examine the exposed surface — cut away circling roots and gently tease out some of the roots at the sides, but do not break up the soil ball. Fill the space between the soil ball and the sides of the hole with planting mixture. Firm down the planting mixture with your hands

(4) After planting there should be a shallow water-holding basin. Water in after planting

BARE-ROOTED PLANT

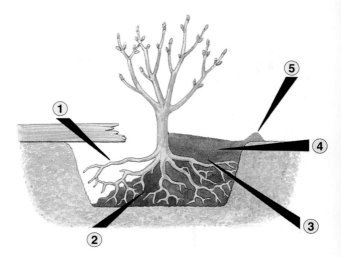

(1) Set a board across the top of the hole — hold the plant against the board and check that the hole is the right size. It should be deep enough to allow the old soil mark on the stem or stems to be at or just below the soil surface. It should be wide enough to allow the roots to be spread out evenly. The specimen should have been prepared for planting by following the instructions on page 109

(2) Work a couple of trowelfuls of planting mixture around the roots. Shake the plant gently up and down — add a little more planting mixture and firm around the roots with your fists

(3) Half-fill the hole with more planting mixture and firm it down by gentle treading. On no account should you stamp heavily. Start treading at the outer edge of the hole and work gradually inwards

(4) Add more planting mixture until the hole is full. Tread down once again and then loosen the surface. Spread a little soil around the stem so that a low dome is formed

(5) Build a shallow ridge of soil around the hole when planting is finished. This will form a water-retaining basin. Water in after planting

STAKING

Note that the information on staking is included in the Planting section. This is the time to secure a tree or tall shrub and not when it has been dislodged or blown over by strong winds. Driving in a stake next to the stem is the traditional way to secure a tree but it is not recommended for container-grown plants as the soil ball would be disturbed. It is better to use the angled stake method illustrated below.

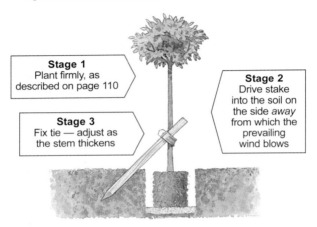

Stage 1
Plant firmly, as described on page 110

Stage 2
Drive stake into the soil on the side *away* from which the prevailing wind blows

Stage 3
Fix tie — adjust as the stem thickens

This method is not practical for a tree or shrub with foliage coming down to ground level. The recommended method here is to use three stout wires as shown below — these wires are secured to three posts and they are cushioned around the stem with short pieces of tubing or garden hose.

CHAPTER 5

PLANT CARE

CARE AFTER PLANTING

Once the new tree or shrub is in place it should be watered in thoroughly. Cut back the branches of bare-rooted plants to about two-thirds of their length — container-grown and balled plants should not need trimming. Evergreens may need extra care. Winter browning of the foliage can take place when they are planted in autumn and so it is a wise precaution to protect choice specimens with a polythene screen (see page 117). When spring arrives, spray the leaves with water on warm days and mulch around the stems.

WATERING

The battle against water shortage should begin before the dry days of summer. Add organic matter to the soil before planting, water in thoroughly after planting and mulch the plant in spring every year.

For the first couple of years of a tree or shrub's life in your garden, copious watering will be necessary during a prolonged dry spell in late spring or summer. Once established the plant will need watering much less often.

The need to water, however, cannot be ignored. If the weather is dry, look at the trouble spots. Climbers growing next to the house, shrubs in tubs and all plants growing in light sandy soil will probably need watering. Then there are the shallow-rooted plants which can quite quickly suffer even in good soil once the dry spells of summer arrive. Rhododendron is a well-known example of a shrub which quickly suffers in drought, but there are many others.

Once you decide to water, then water thoroughly — a light sprinkling can do more harm than good. As a rough guide use 5 litres for each small shrub and 20 litres for each large one. A watering can is often used, but a hose-pipe is a much better idea unless your garden is very small. Remember to water slowly close to the base of the plant.

Trickle irrigation through a perforated hose laid close to the bushes is perhaps the best method of watering. A quick and easy technique popular in America is to build a ridge of soil around each bush and then fill the basin with a hose.

FEEDING

The production of stems, leaves and flowers is a drain on the soil's reserves of nitrogen, phosphates, potash and other nutrients. However the extensive root system of an established shrub can effectively tap the resources in the soil, which means that regular feeding is not usually necessary. The routine followed by many gardeners is to apply a balanced fertilizer such as Growmore to the soil around shrubs and trees every two or three years.

Shrubs with large flower-heads and/or a prolonged flowering season do need feeding at least once a year. Use a potash-rich fertilizer, such as a proprietary rose food. Remember that shrubs should not be fed after the end of July.

A few rules. The soil should be moist before feeding — water first if the soil is dry. Use no more than the recommended amount and keep solid fertilizers off leaves and flowers.

MULCHING

The benefits of using an organic mulch in the spring are numerous and remarkable, but most gardeners still do not bother to mulch their shrubs. There are five basic reasons for using this underrated technique:

- The soil below is kept moist during the dry days of summer.
- The soil surface is kept cool during the hot days of summer. This moist and cool root zone promotes more active growth than in unmulched areas.
- Annual weeds are kept in check — the ones that do appear can be easily pulled out.
- Some mulches provide plant foods.
- Soil structure is improved by the addition of humus.

The standard time for mulching is May. Success depends on preparing the soil surface properly before adding the organic blanket. Remove debris, dead leaves and weeds, and then water the surface if it is dry. Apply a spring feed if this has not been done, hoe in lightly and you are now ready to apply the mulch. Spread a 5-8 cm layer over the area which is under the branches and leaves. Do not take the mulch right up to the stems — a build-up of moist organic matter around the base may lead to rotting. In October lightly fork this dressing into the top 2 cm of soil — replace in spring.

MULCHING MATERIALS

Peat: Widely available, but blows about when dry

Bark: A better choice than peat — lasts for 2-3 years

Well-rotted manure: Inexpensive — the best soil improver

Garden compost: Free — renew annually

TRY TO PREVENT WEEDS FROM APPEARING The basic reason why you have a weed problem is bare ground. You can hoe or hand pull the weeds around growing plants and in some cases they can be safely sprayed, but if the soil is uncovered then the problem will return as weed seeds on or near the surface and pieces of perennial weeds start to grow. Digging is often an ineffectual way of controlling weeds on a long term basis. The annual types on the surface are buried, but a host of seeds are brought to the surface. With care some perennial weed roots and bulbs can be removed, but all too often the roots of dandelions, thistles etc and the bulbs of ground elder are spread around. The real answer is to try to cover the surface around plants in beds and borders. You can use a non-living cover (a mulch or weed-proof blanket) or a living one (ground-cover plants). Use one of the following techniques:

Apply a non-living cover One of the purposes of a humus mulch (see page 114) is to suppress weed germination and to make it easier to hand pull ones which may appear. This reduces but does not eliminate the problem. Plastic sheeting provides a complete answer — cover with bark.

Plant ground cover Creeping evergreens with leafy stems provide an excellent way of suppressing weed growth around clumps of perennials. With bedding plants you can solve the ground cover problem by planting them closer together than the usually recommended distance.

GET RID OF WEEDS PROMPTLY WHEN THEY APPEAR Weeds will appear around your plants in beds or borders unless you have put some form of weed-proof blanket such as plastic sheeting around them. These weeds should be kept in check while they are still small. Use one or more of the methods listed below:

Pull by hand The simplest method for the removal of well-established but easily-uprooted annual weeds in beds and borders and the removal of all types of weeds in the rockery.

Use a hoe The hoe is the traditional enemy of the emerged weed. It will kill large numbers of annual weeds if the surface is dry, the blade is sharp and the cut is kept shallow. Hoeing at regular intervals is needed for perennial weeds.

Use a weedkiller Numerous weedkillers are available for use around growing plants. Make sure you use the right type — check the label.

TRAINING & SUPPORTING

Supporting and training are not quite the same thing. Supporting involves the provision of a post, stake or framework to which weak stems can be attached. Training involves the fixing of branches into desired positions so that an unnatural but desirable growth habit is produced.

Some shrubs with lax spreading stems may require some means of support after a few years. Use 3 or 4 stakes with a band joining the top of each stake — never rely on a single pole and twine.

Climbers must be grown against a support from the outset to ensure that they remain attached to it and grow in the desired direction. Use trellis work, posts, pillars, pergolas, fences etc. Make sure that all fence posts are well-anchored. For covering walls use plastic-covered straining wire stretched horizontally at 45 cm intervals — there should be at least 8 cm between the wire and the wall.

Many plants can be grown against walls in this way, including weak-stemmed non-climbers such as Jasminum nudiflorum and Forsythia suspensa. The wire ties used to attach the main stems to the supports should not be tied too tightly. Plant the climber about 30-45 cm away from the base of the wall. When growing climbers up a pillar, wind the stems in an ascending spiral (see illustration) rather than attaching to one side of the support.

The main stems need not all be trained vertically — spreading them horizontally to form an espalier or at an angle to form a fan can dramatically increase the floral display.

CUTTING & DEAD-HEADING

Cutting blooms and attractive foliage from shrubs for arranging indoors is, of course, a basic part of the gardening scene. This form of spring and summer pruning generally does no harm, but take care during the first year after planting. A newly-planted shrub needs all the stems and green leaves it can produce, so only cut a few of the flowers and do not remove many leaves.

The removal of dead flowers has several advantages — it keeps the bush tidy, it may prolong the flowering season and in a few cases it may induce a second flush later in the season. It is impractical to dead-head most shrubs, but it is necessary with large flower-heads such as Lilac and Buddleia. Do not remove the faded flower-heads of Hydrangea until March. The dead flowers of Rhododendron should be carefully broken off with finger and thumb.

FIRMING

Some of the techniques in this chapter are practised by all gardeners — watering, pruning etc, but firming is generally the sign of an experienced gardener. During the winter months strong winds can disturb newly-planted shrubs and shallow-rooted ones such as Escallonia. This windrock causes a gap to appear in the soil around the roots, and water collects here when the heavy spring rains fall. The situation can be made worse by the soil heave caused by frost. To combat the effect of these root-disturbing agents you should firm the soil in spring — gently tread down the soil above the root zone of shrubs which have worked loose during the winter. Wait until the soil is fairly dry before doing this job.

WINTER PROTECTION

The snow and frost of an average winter usually do little or no harm to the shrubs in the garden, but an abnormally severe winter can cause losses. With types which are not fully hardy, the base of the shrub should be covered with a blanket of straw or peat. Newly-planted stock will benefit from some form of frost protection, especially if it is evergreen and known to be rather tender. Build a plastic screen — make sure that the bottom of the plastic sheeting is pinned down to prevent draughts.

Established plants are more resistant than newly-planted ones to frost, but they are more liable to damage by the other winter enemy — snow. The weight on large branches can cause them to break. If heavy snow is forecast it may be worth tying the branches of a choice evergreen with twine, but it is usually not necessary — just gently shake the branches to remove most of the snow.

PRUNING

Pruning has a very simple meaning — the cutting away of unwanted growth from woody plants. But the purpose of pruning is less easy to understand, as there is nearly always more than one reason for carrying out this work:

- To remove poor quality wood, such as weak twigs, dead or diseased branches and damaged shoots.
- To shape the shrub to your needs. This calls for the removal of healthy but unwanted wood — examples include the removal of a minor branch which is rubbing against a major one and the cutting back of branches which are blocking a pathway or growing into neighbouring shrubs.
- To regulate both the quality and quantity of blossom and/or fruit production.

The craft of pruning is perhaps the most difficult lesson the gardener has to learn. Both the timing and the technique depend on the age and type of the tree or shrub. If you are a novice you must check carefully the rules for the particular plant you wish to tackle. The table below is only a general guide and you should consult the A-Z section for instructions relating to individual trees and shrubs.

TIMING

The correct time for pruning each tree or shrub is given in the A-Z section. There are no general rules, but a guide to pruning some popular groups is given below. Note, however, that there are numerous exceptions.

DECIDUOUS TREES AND SHRUBS WHICH BLOOM BEFORE THE END OF MAY
Cut out weak, dead and awkwardly-placed shoots. Remove overcrowded branches. Finally, cut back all the branches which have borne blooms. Time to prune: As soon as flowering has finished — do not delay

DECIDUOUS TREES AND SHRUBS WHICH BLOOM AFTER THE END OF MAY
Cut out weak, dead and awkwardly-placed shoots. Remove overcrowded branches. Finally, cut back hard all old wood. Time to prune: January-March — do not wait until growth starts

EVERGREEN TREES AND SHRUBS
Cut out weak, dead and awkwardly-placed shoots. Remove overcrowded branches. Time to prune: May

HEDGES
See page 122

SPECIMEN CONIFERS
Avoid pruning if possible

TYPES OF PRUNING

STANDARD PRUNING The partial removal of the woody structure of the plant, each cut being made individually. In some cases hardly any wood is removed (light pruning) but in others a significant proportion of the stems and branches are cut away (hard pruning).

SHEARING The partial removal of the woody structure of the plant, the cuts being made in wholesale fashion with garden shears or an electric hedge trimmer. This is the method of producing topiary (a decorative-shaped shrub) or a formal hedge.

STOOLING The complete removal of the woody structure of the plant. Some shrubs can be pruned back each spring to almost ground level — examples include Romneya, Fuchsia, Caryopteris and Spiraea japonica. This type of pruning is known as coppicing in forestry.

LOPPING The removal of a large branch from a main stem — only applies to trees and large shrubs which have become tree-like with age. Make a shallow saw-cut on the underside of the branch before sawing downwards.

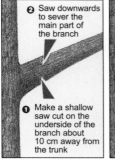

❷ Saw downwards to sever the main part of the branch

❶ Make a shallow saw cut on the underside of the branch about 10 cm away from the trunk

Saw off the stub — make the cut almost flush with the trunk

Pare away the rough edges with a pruning knife

BASIC TOOLS

TWO-BLADED SECATEURS
will cut cleanly for many years with proper care. The cut must be made at the centre of the blades — maximum diameter 1.5-2 cm

LONG-HANDLED PRUNER
for stems 1.5-4 cm across — many gardeners prefer them to a pruning saw for dealing with thick stems. Essential for tall shrubs and trees

GARDEN SHEARS
are required for trimming hedges and tidying-up in the border. Buy a good pair and make sure they are properly set — keep them clean, dry and sharp

ELECTRIC HEDGE TRIMMER
will take the hard work out of hedge trimming — a good buy if you have a large stretch to keep under control. Take care — read the instructions and precautions before you start

PRUNING SAW
is useful if you have stems over 1.5 cm across to be cut

PRUNING RULES

- Use good quality tools and make sure they are sharp.
- Cut out all diseased, dead and weak growth. Always prune back to healthy wood, free from the tell-tale staining of infected tissue.
- When pruning any woody plant, realise the difference between light and hard pruning. Light pruning results in **heading back** — the tips of the branches are removed and this stimulates the buds below to burst into growth. The long-term effect is to produce a plant which is smaller but denser than one left unpruned. This technique is used for formal shaping. Hard pruning results in **thinning** — entire branches are removed back to the main stem and energy is diverted to the remaining branches. The long-term effect is to produce a plant which is larger but more open than one left unpruned. This technique is used for informal shaping.
- If you are a beginner in the craft of pruning do not attempt any drastic treatment. Too little pruning of healthy wood is safer than too much.
- Collect up all prunings. Compost them if they are soft and healthy — burn them if they are woody or diseased.
- All cuts must be clean. Pare off ragged parts left on sawn surfaces.

HEADING BACK **THINNING**

THE PRUNING CUT

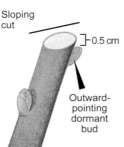

Sloping cut

0.5 cm

Outward-pointing dormant bud

When dealing with a few large branches it is worth while taking the trouble to use the classic pruning cut. It is not possible to avoid making some wrong cuts — as a result snags of dead wood will form above new shoots. Cut off these dead bits. With smaller multi-stemmed shrubs it may not be practical to attempt the recommended pruning cut as each branch is shortened.

CHAPTER 6

HEDGING

The usual reason for planting a hedge is to form a boundary between you and the road or your neighbour. It must be capable of providing some privacy and also a degree of protection against dogs, children etc. There are other roles a hedge can play — it can divide one area of the garden from another, it can edge beds and borders, and also serve as a screen against unsightly views and noise.

The one-variety hedge is standard, but there are variations. With a privet or holly hedge you can mix an all-green variety with a variegated one or you can grow two or more quite different hedging plants to produce a tapestry hedge.

HEDGE TYPES

Formal Hedge

This is the traditional hedge, densely clothed with leaves and pruned to form a smooth surface. A few types do bear flowers or berries but they are generally grown for their leafiness and impermeability.

Informal Hedge

This includes the flowering and the berrying hedge which are not pruned to provide a smooth surface, as this would reduce or prevent the floral display. Some privacy is provided, but this is not usually its main purpose.

Dwarf Hedge

This is the edging hedge used to divide beds and borders within the garden. The plants are kept at 90 cm or less by regular pruning — naturally low-growing plants can be grown as an informal hedge.

CHOOSING A HEDGE

The job a hedge has to do is a vital factor in the correct choice of planting material — so is the degree of formality required and the desired height. The blessings of a tall and dense hedge for privacy are obvious, but do consider the drawbacks. If it is to serve as a boundary do discuss it with your neighbour before going ahead — over-vigorous boundary hedges are one of the commonest causes of disputes. Also think about the effect on your own garden — shade will be a problem for nearby plants and so will the drain on both the water and nutrient resources in the soil.

Formal Hedging

Carpinus (Hornbeam): Similar to beech, but more reliable in heavy soil. Trim in August.

Crataegus (Hawthorn): Untidy on its own — grow as a mixed hedge with privet, holly etc.

Cupressocyparis (Cypress): C. leylandii is the quickest-growing of all hedges. Trim twice a year.

Fagus (Beech): Deciduous, but brown leaves remain over winter. Tolerates chalky soil. Trim in August.

Ilex (Holly): Good in shade, but variegated types need some sun. Trim in August.

Ligustrum (Privet): Much despised, but it is quick-growing and tolerant of poor conditions.

Prunus (Laurel): Fine tall hedge with large shiny leaves — needs space. Trim in August.

Taxus (Yew): Slow but not dull if you choose a golden variety. Trim in August.

Informal Hedging

Berberis (Barberry): Several species make fine hedges. Yellow flowers in spring — trim when they fade.

Escallonia (Escallonia): Popular in coastal areas. Red flowers in June — trim when they fade.

Pyracantha (Firethorn): P. rogersiana recommended for hedging. Trim in August to expose berries.

Rhododendron (Rhododendron): R. ponticum needs acid soil and space. Trim when blooms fade.

Spiraea (Spiraea): S. vanhouttei has arching branches and May flowers — trim when they fade.

Viburnum (Viburnum): V. tinus provides winter flowers on difficult sites — trim in May.

Dwarf Hedging

Buxus (Box): An old favourite for dwarf hedging. Slow growing. Trim in July/August.

Lavandula (Lavender): Popular aromatic hedge. Dead-head in late summer, trim in late April.

Rosmarinus (Rosemary): Not as reliable as lavender. Small flowers in spring — trim when they fade.

Santolina (Cotton Lavender): Silvery foliage. Dead-head in late summer, trim in late April.

PLANTING A HEDGE

Having decided on the area for planting, dig a 90 cm wide strip to house the plants. Remove the roots of perennial weeds and then mark out the position of the planting holes. Single row planting is recommended where economy is an important factor and quick cover is not essential. Mark out the planting line with string stretched along the centre of the cultivated area and use canes to mark out the planting sites. Set the canes 40-45 cm apart for shrubs such as privet and 60-75 cm for large shrubs and trees.

Double row planting is recommended for spindly shrubs and where maximum cover is required as quickly as possible. Use string to mark out the planting lines 40 cm apart and put in the canes at 45 cm intervals along these lines.

Plant out as described on pages 110-111. Stretch a wire tightly along the young plants and attach them with ties. Keep the plants well watered during the first season.

PRUNING A HEDGE

For a formal hedge it is essential to build up a plentiful supply of shoots at the base. This calls for hard pruning shortly after planting — cut back the plants to about ⅔ of their original height. Do not prune again during the first growing season.

In the second year clip lightly on three or four occasions between May and August. Do not leave it untrimmed because it has not yet reached the required height — the purpose of this second year pruning is to increase shoot density and to create the desired shape before the ultimate height is reached. Use a pair of shears or an electric hedge trimmer. Lay down a sheet of plastic at the base — this will make the removal of fallen clippings a much easier task.

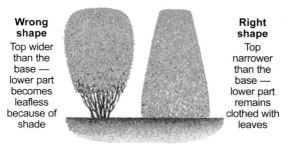

Wrong shape
Top wider than the base — lower part becomes leafless because of shade

Right shape
Top narrower than the base — lower part remains clothed with leaves

Once the hedge has reached the desired height, trimming should take place between May and August each year (unless otherwise stated on page 122) when the plants look untidy. This may involve a single clipping during the season or trimming every 6 weeks to maintain a neatly manicured box hedge. Cut back to a little above the last cut, leaving about 1 cm of new growth.

CHAPTER 7
PLANT INDEX

Acknowledgements

The author wishes to acknowledge the painstaking work of
Gill Jackson and Angelina Gibbs. Grateful acknowledgement is
also made for the help received from Joan Hessayon, Colin Bailey,
Ella Norris, Brian O'Shea and Barry Highland (Spot On Digital
Imaging Ltd). The author is also grateful for the photographs and/or
artworks received from Harry Smith Horticultural Photographic
Collection, Pat Brindley and Christine Wilson.

The Experts —
the world's best-selling gardening books

The Bedding Plant Expert
The Bulb Expert
The Container Expert
The Easy-care Gardening Expert
The Evergreen Expert
The Flower Arranging Expert
The Flower Expert
The Flowering Shrub Expert
The Fruit Expert
The Garden Expert
The Garden DIY Expert
The Greenhouse Expert
The House Plant Expert
The Lawn Expert
The Rock & Water Garden Expert
The Rose Expert
The Tree & Shrub Expert
The Vegetable & Herb Expert

The FLOWERING SHRUB EXPERT

The HOUSE PLANT EXPERT
Dr. D. G. Hessayon

The TREE & SHRU EXPERT
Dr. D. G. Hessayon

The ROSE EXPERT

The NEW FLOWER EXPERT
Dr. D. G. Hessayon

The GARDEN DIY EXPERT
Dr. D. G. Hessayon

The BEDDING PLANT EXPERT
Dr. D. G. Hessayon

The GARDEN EXPERT
Dr. D. G. Hessayon

The EVERGREEN EXPERT
Dr. D. G. Hessayon

The LAWN EXPERT
Dr. D. G. Hessayon

The GREENHOUSE EXPERT
Dr. D. G. Hessayon

The BULB EXPERT
Dr. D. G. Hessayon

The EASY-CARE GARDENING EXPERT Dr. D. G. Hessayon

The ROCK & WATER GARDEN EXPERT

The CONTAINER EXPERT
Dr. D. G. Hessayon

The VEGETABLE & HERB EXPERT
Dr. D. G. Hessayon

The FRUIT EXPERT
Dr. D. G. Hessayon

The FLOWER ARRANGING EXPERT